A. R. HOGUE

Author "History of Putnam County," "School Improvement Club,"
"Twenty-five Lessons in Quick Figuring."

HISTORY

of

FENTRESS COUNTY TENNESSEE

THE OLD HOME OF MARK TWAIN'S ANCESTORS

Press of
Williams Printing Co., Nashville, Tenn.
1916

Notice

In many older books, foxing (or discoloration) occurs and, in some instances, print lightens with wear and age. Reprinted books, such as this, often duplicate these flaws, notwithstanding efforts to reduce or eliminate them. The pages of this reprint have been digitally enhanced and, where possible, the flaws eliminated in order to provide clarity of content and a pleasant reading experience.

Originally published
Nashville
1916

Reprinted by:

Janaway Publishing, Inc.
732 Kelsey Ct.
Santa Maria, California 93454
(805) 925-1038
www.janawaygenealogy.com

2010

ISBN: 978-1-59641-220-0

History of Fentress County

INTRODUCTION

FENTRESS COUNTY is a great county in many respects. Few countries furnish grander scenery. Many countries of wide fame have less attraction and less merit than our own county. One will travel far to find more balmy, invigorating breezes than bless this land. This, with the pure, cold, health-giving waters, make this county an ideal place for a home, or for a health resort.

The inhabitants of the county are nearly all pure Caucasian blood, and are descendants of noble ancestry. Some of them are descendants of some of the greatest characters of the nation's history. Fentress County has been represented in every great movement in the State or Nation by some of its citizenry, or by their ancestors.

The purpose of this history is to place before the people of the county and their children a history of the part their county has played in State and national affairs, and to inspire a higher order of citizenship, by acquainting all with what their people have already done, and the readiness they have always displayed in performing their part in affairs which have become historic.

The author regrets that some sketches in this history are very brief, and regrets more that some families are not represented at all on account of the failure of those concerned to furnish the necessary information to make up sketch. The thanks of the author is extended to all who may have in any way contributed to this arduous but pleasant undertaking.

ALBERT R. HOGUE.

CHAPTER I

FENTRESS COUNTY.

FENTRESS COUNTY is located in the northern part of Tennessee, east of the center of the State, and lies principally on the Cumberland Plateau. It originally bordered on Kentucky, but Pickett County was formed partly from its northern territory in 1881.

Fentress County has an area of 486 square miles, or 311,000 acres. It was created by an act of the legislature in session at Murfreesboro in 1823, from territory carved out of Overton County. It was named for James Fentress, a prominent Tennessee legislator for many years, and later an officer in the Confederate army.

Its county seat, Jamestown, is situated near the center of the county on the Cumberland Plateau. The site was no doubt selected on account of the fact that it was near the geographical center of the county, and the fact that several fine springs of water bubble up from the sand here. The place was once called Sand Springs, later it became the Obedstown of the "Gilded Age", by Mark Twain. This place is on an Indian trace and was an Indian resting place on their trips from the east to the Cumberland River region. It also possibly furnished them a camping ground while hunting on the plateau. This region has always been a good range for deer, bear, turkeys, and other wild animals. There are still a few of these animals to be found on the plateau.

When the first courthouse was built, in 1828, there were only five families living in the town. Their names are given elsewhere in this book. The town was incorporated in 1837. The act of incorporation was not repealed until a few years ago. Its growth has been slow until within the past few years. The population of the town, according to the census of 1910, was 350. All are white. This is practically t r u e of the entire county, there being only ninety-eight colored people in the county, and 7,348 white.

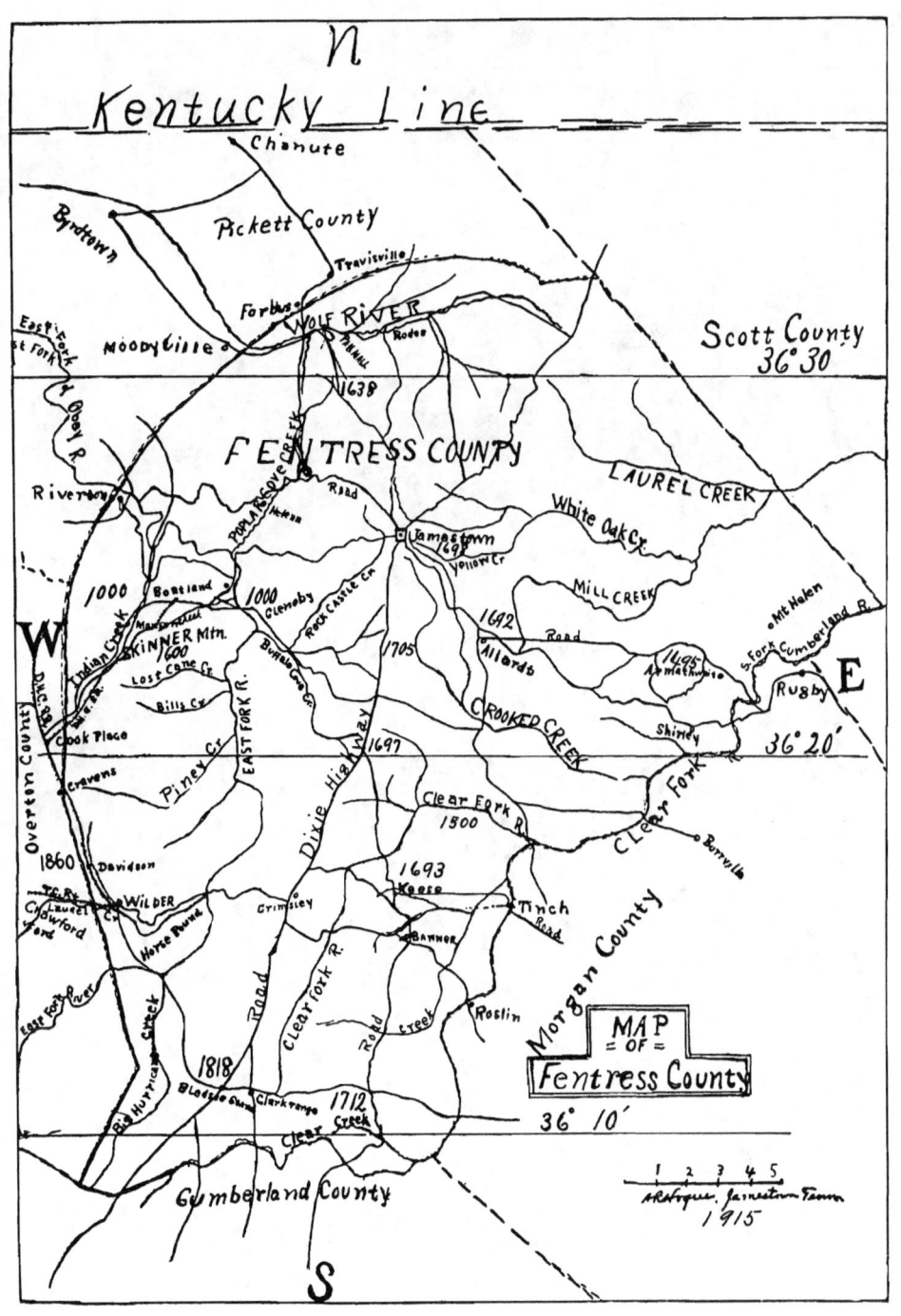

LOGGING—MOUTH OF INDIAN CREEK

CEDAR RAFTS ON EAST FORK, GLENOBY

CHAPTER II

SURFACE AND AREA.

THE area of Fentress County, according to the census of 1910, is 311,040 acres. The surface presents a great variety of features. The greater part lies on the Cumberland Plateau. This part is practically level. There is also considerable level land in the East Fork and the Wolf River valleys. These are the three principal natural divisions of the county.

The western part of the county is broken by many small streams. The East Fork, the most important stream, flows from south to north through this part. High cliffs and peaks and deep hollows are common. Wolf River flows across the northern part.

SOIL.

The soil of the county is usually fertile, and produces good crops without the use of fertilizers. This is especially true of the valleys.

The soil of the plateau is sandy, and is quite easily cultivated, and yields large returns when properly cultivated.

Among others, W. J. Gaudin has successfully and fully demonstrated the great possibilities of the plateau as a farming area. In 1913 he sold 7,200 pounds of watermelons at one cent a pound from a little over a half acre, after using a part of the crop for the family and neighbors and feeding a great many to his stock. He probably raised 10,000 pounds on the lot. The same year he gathered fifty bushels of first-class onions from one-eighth of an acre.

He raised forty bushels of corn to the acre on a tract of land that had been in corn the two years previous.

In 1912 he dug and cellared 202 bushels of fine Irish potatoes from three-fourths of an acre. He used very little commercial fertilizers. His land is typical Cumberland Mountain land.

All the cereals and legumes have been produced successfully on the plateau.

The Germans at Allardt have demonstrated this land to be suited to horticulture as well as general farming.

One of the great natural advantages of the plateau is the fine wild grass which grows so abundantly during the spring and summer. Twenty-five thousand head of cattle could be fattened on this range every summer.

Good water for man and beast abounds everywhere.

Lumbering is an important industry of the plateau, as well as in other parts of the county. Fifteen carloads were recently shipped from here to Canada. Nashville, however, is the leading market for logs and lumber from this section.

The forests contain nearly all the varieties of hardwood. Poplar, cedar, cherry and walnut are found principally in the valleys.

WOLF RIVER.

The Wolf River region is one of the finest farming regions in the State. It also contains some of the finest forests of timber in the South.

This valley was once popularly called the heart of Fentress County. It was then the source of supply for agricultural products for many parts of the county. At that time the mountain people were engaged in shipping tar, turpentine and rosin, and paid little attention to farming.

FIRST SETTLERS.

Among the pioneers in this valley were Coonrod Pile, Pearson Miller, Arthur Frogge, John Riley and Moses Poor.

Pearson Miller, one of these pioneers, baked his bread on a hoe and drank his milk from a terrapin shell in regular pioneer fashion.

The first county court ever held in this county met in the Horseshoe Bend of Wolf River.

EAST FORK OF OBEY'S RIVER.

Obey's River is said to have been named by the "Long Hunters" in honor of one of their number—Obadiah Terrill. (One of these hunters—Bob Crockett—was killed by the Indians in Overton, an adjoining county.)

The East Fork is a very rapid stream and would furnish an immense amount of water power if harnessed. Thousands of logs are carried down the river every winter to the Cumberland and to Nashville, where they are marketed.

For many years this has been the chief source to supply money to the people. Stock raising and other farm products are taking the place of the timber industry and proving more profitable to the people generally.

ROCK CASTLE.

Rock Castle Creek rises near Jamestown and drops over a high cliff about one and a half miles southwest of Jamestown with a roar that can be heard for a long distance.

Rock Castle is almost surrounded by precipitous walls of rock. In this natural enclosure cattle, sheep and hogs thrive and fatten on grasses, acorns and various nuts that abound.

The Castle also contains fine coal and timber.

The falls and Cudjo's Cave are two of the many natural curiosities in this valley.

In concluding this geographical description, in which only the principal natural divisions of the county have been mentioned, it may be said that the county is rich in coal, and has some iron, oil and gas. Several paying oil wells have been struck by drillers. Other minerals have also been found. The author regrets that he must at this time omit further details of the resources of this great county. Later he hopes to publish in another volume a complete geology and geography of the county.

CHAPTER III

AN HISTORIC TOWN.

JAMESTOWN, COUNTY SEAT OF FENTRESS COUNTY, AND ITS PECULIARITIES.—AWAKENING FROM A RIP VAN WINKLE SLUMBER.—A CHURCH BEING BUILT, THE FIRST IN OVER SIXTY YEARS.

JAMESTOWN, TENN., March 17, 1893.

A HORSEBACK ride through the mountain county affords the best means for examining the undeveloped resources of this part of the State, and at the same time giving an insight into the real home life of the people not to be obtained in any other way. Such a ride will give a glimpse of many strange nooks and corners never discovered by the regular tourist. One may pass through a number of quaint old towns, which have seemingly remained unchanged since the days of Jackson, when the stage coaches, with their loads of dusty passengers, rumbled up to the doors of the same old tavern which is still the resting place of the tired traveler. Such a town is Jamestown, the county seat of Fentress County, familiarly called Jimtown. It is one of the oldest towns in the State, and until the last twelve months, was also generally regarded by the outside world as the deadest.

It is said for the past sixty years the sound of the hammer or saw has not been heard there, and not a single nail has been driven into any new building. Only about a year ago a visitor would have seen nothing but historic old buildings. One of them, the former home of the parents of Mark Twain, whose book, the "Gilded Age", describes the town and the surrounding country as it then appeared.

The old brick courthouse, with its large yard and tall pine trees, the ancient jail, which from its very age should command the respect of evil doers; the curious old store and hotel of Uncle Wade Ervin, renowned throughout all the mountain country, and most of the other old buildings are still there.

But a great change has already taken place in the town, and other changes are rapidly following, so that perhaps in another twelve months the old landmarks will have almost disappeared. Some of the old buildings have been improved and remodeled. Modern houses are going up, the business houses are being enlarged and improved, and the old town will soon lose many of the relics of antiquity to which it has clung so long

The most important building now going up is the Masonic Hall, which will be one of the finest buildings in this section. It is to be nearly forty feet by seventy, two stories, each fourteen feet in height. The lower floor will be used as a church, the upper floor being reserved for a lodge room. The walls will be panelled in ten-foot squares, each panel to be of different variety of native wood finished in the natural color.

The building is located on a beautiful knoll just at the edge of the old town and a fine view will be obtained of the town. The work on the building is well under way, and the committee in charge intend to have it completed by the last of June, when it is to be dedicated by the Masonic lodges of Fentress and neighboring counties with appropriate ceremonies.

The building is to cost about three thousand dollars when completed. The people of Jamestown deserve credit for their enterprise in erecting such a building.

The business men of the town seem a live, progressive lot of very clever men, and one is led to wonder why the town has been allowed to lie asleep so many years. This has been due to its situation remote from railroads or any but the most primitive means of transportation, which has discouraged everyone from any attempt at improvement.

The old Ervin House is always pointed out to the visitor as one of the curiosities of the town. It is in some one of the many buildings which comprise this ancient hostelry that Mark Twain passed some years of his boyhood, but which particular houses or room was the one occupied by the celebrated author seems to be one of the things past finding out.

The hotel consists of fifteen or twenty small houses—some log and some frame—all of them very old, which have been built at different times, and are joined together by a number of covered passageways and dark corriders in which one almost needs a guide.

Mr. Ervin (Uncle Wade, as he is known far and wide), keeps a general store in one end of this building, which in itself would be worth a long ride to see.

Many stories are told of the proprietor's eccentricities, but for all that, he is a genial old gentleman, who sticks to his old-fashioned ways, and has many interesting stories to tell of the good old times.

There are several other stores, and a steam saw mill lately located here seems to be doing a thriving business. A weekly newspaper, started nearly a year ago, has already become one of the fixtures, and will no doubt strive to create a boom for the town. Among the improvements talked of for the coming summer are a new stone jail, some repairs for the moss-grown courthouse, and many private dwellings.

The survey of the N. & K. railroad is watched with the greatest interest by the citizens who hope to see it built to within fifteen miles of the town. At present the nearest railroad point is Sedgmoor on the Cincinnati Southern.

Already one hears considerable talk of the present and prospective values of real estate, and some of the most sanguine holders of town lots are prepared to advise speedy purchases, assuring the prospective customers, like Col. Mulberry Sellers, that "There is millions in it."

The above article, which appeared in the *Chattanooga Times* March 29, 1893, was furnished the author by Mrs. Maggie Burns, a niece of Wade Ervin. It serves to show how visitors have been impressed with the town, and furnishes some history. The writer was mistaken in regard to Mark Twain having spent part of his boyhood here. His parents left here a few months before Mark was born.

The church building was completed on time. The Masons and the Odd Fellows use the upper floor, the lower floor is used by the church. The Baptist's are building a nice church in the corner of the lot just north of the present church.

Within the past few years many nice residences have been built. Among them are the following: Judge W. R. Case,

Supt. W. E. Mullinix, Mrs. Ada Sussner, M. F. Hurst, Capt. E. M. Shelley, Register B. L. Brier, W. J. Gaudin and Travis Smith. The county has also erected a nice building on the Poor Farm north of town. B. A. Greer, Mark Greer, B. F. Voils and Sylvanus Crowley have also erected nice buildings, and there are perhaps others.

A high school building, costing over three thousand dollars, has been built and equipped with modern equipment.

A courthouse and jail of native stone have been built within the past few years. Both are modern up-to-date buildings in appearance as well as service and durability.

A first-class hotel has been provided for the traveling public by the proprietor, W. M. Johnson. It is called the Mark Twain House, this being the second to go by that name.

CHAPTER IV

JOHN M. CLEMONS' PLAN FOR A COURTHOUSE AND JAIL—1827.

REV. J. L. GARRETT has in his possession the original draft of plans and specifications for the first courthouse and jail ever built in Fentress County. It was written by John M. Clemons, one of the commissioners. He was the father of Mark Twain. The following is a copy of plan presented to the county court:

The Commissioners of the Town of Jamestown prepare the following as descriptions of the public buildings to be let to the lowest bidder on Tuesday the 20th day of March 1827 to wit, for a jail, a house of loggs hewed a foot square, twelve feet in the clear, two stories high, and this surrounded by another wall precisely of the same description, with a space between the two walls of about eight or ten inches, and that space filled completely with scinned hickory poles, the ground floor to be formed of sills hewed about a foot square and laid closely, the second floor to be formed of two sets of logs of the same description and laid transversely, and the third or upper floor to be the same as the first, the logs composing each of the floors to extend through the inner wall of the building, and those composing the upper floor to extend across both walls and set on the outside ones as girders, a good substantial shingle roof, two small windows strongly grated to the lower room, to the upper room one outer door, with three shutters fixed with locks bars &c. in the most substantial manner, with two windows each at least two feet square to the upper room, also strongly grated, and a trap door to go down from the upper into the lower room, with a strong shutter and a lock, all the locks to be of the strongest and best description in common use for jails, and to be completed by the first day of May 1828, the inner wall of the jail may be of pine, but the other must be of chestnut or more durable wood. Mill stairs to the doors on the outside.

WINTER SCENE IN ROCK CASTLE

For the courthouse they will offer both of the following descriptions to be bid for, reserving to themselves the right of choosing which they will take after the bids are made, to wit, for the one they propose a one story brick house 40 feet long and 27 feet wide in the clear with a brick partition across so as to make a court room thirty feet square, and another brick partition running from the middle of the other to the end of the house so as to form two jury rooms thirteen and one half by ten feet each, one chimney with a fireplace in each of the jury rooms in the corner. Doors, One door to each jury room opening into the court room, two outer doors one on each side about the center of the building—the court bench to be situated at the opposite ends from the jury rooms, and to be put up as well as the bar, Sheriff and clerk's boxes, jury benches &c. all in good stile, and finished in a workmanlike manner, two windows in the end over the court bench, one on each side, over the sheriff boxes, and one to each jury room, all of the usual size filled with glass 10 by 12, and shutters. A good shingle roof to be painted and all the wood work to be painted of suitable colours and the inside plaistered, a brick floor to all the rooms, the house from the floor to the ceiling to be fourteen feet high.

The other a hewed log building of the same dimensions and with partition walls, fireplaces, doors a n d windows as described for the brick building—a shingle roof—the floor to be formed of large timber say eight inches thick, the walls pinted with lime, all the joiner work to be in about the same order as described in the other building, except that it is not to be painted, whichever building the commissioners may prefer is to be completed by the first day of May 1828.

P. S. A foundation to the brick house to be laid of rock on a solid foundation under the surface and raised so high as to be of the height of eighteen inches above the surface of the ground at the highest part—the walls to be 18 inches thick, the partition structure of the bar, clerks and sheriffs boxes &c to be under the particular direction of t h e Commissioners hereafter, or if no directions to be on the plan of t h o s e at Gainesborough.

CHAPTER V

MARK TWAIN'S DESCRIPTION OF JAMESTOWN AND THE SURROUNDINGS.

SQUIRE HAWKINS sat upon the pyramid of large blocks called the stile, in front of his house, contemplating the morning. The locality was Obedstown, East Tennessee. You would not know that Obedstown stood on the top of a mountain for there was nothing about the landscape to indicate it—but it did. A mountain that stretched abroad over whole counties and rose very gradually. The district was called the Knobs of East Tennessee and had a reputation like Nazareth, as far as turning out any good thing was concerned.

The Squire's house was a double log cabin in a state of decay; two or three gaunt hounds lay asleep about the threshold, and lifted their heads sadly whenever Mrs. Hawkins, or the children, stepped in or out over their bodies.

Rubbish was scattered about the grassless yard, a bench stood near the door with a tin wash basin on it, and a pail of water and a gourd; a cat had begun to drink from the pail, but the exertion was overtaxing her energies, and she had stopped to rest. There was an ash hopper by the fence and an iron pot for soft soap boiling near it.

This dwelling constituted one-fifteenth of Obedstown. The other fourteen houses were scattered among the tall pine trees, and among the cornfields in such a way that a man might stand in the midst of the city and not know but that he was in the country, if he only depended on his eyes for information.

Squire Hawkins got his title from being postmaster of Obedstown—not that the title belongs to the office, but because in those regions the chief citizens always must have titles of some sort, and so the usual courtesy had been extended to Hawkins.

The mail was monthly and sometimes amounted to as much as three or four letters at a single delivery. Even a rush like this did not fill up a postmaster's whole month, though, and therefore he kept store in the intervals. * * * * (The next few pages of "Gilded Age" describes a scene at the post-office, where all the citizens of the town are represented as waiting for the mail. Hawkins receives a letter from a friend asking him to come at once to Missouri, which is described as "the grandest country, the loveliest land," etc. Later he tells his wife of his intention to buy a wagon and team, put her and the children in it and move to Missouri, but tells his wife he has a fortune awaiting his children in land that he had taken up in the country.)

"Do you see these papers? Well, they are evidence that I have taken up seventy-five thousand acres of l a n d in this county—think what an enormous fortune it will be some day! Why, Nancy, enormous don't express it—the word's too tame! I tell you Nancy—" "For goodness sake, Si—" "Wait, Nancy, wait—let me finish—I've been secretly boiling and fuming with this grand inspiration for weeks, and I must talk or I'll burst! I have not whispered to a soul—not a word—have had my countenance under lock and key, for fear it might drop something that would tell even these animals here how to discern the gold mine that's even glaring under their noses.

"Now, all that's necessary to hold all this land and keep it in the family is to pay the trifling taxes on it yearly—five or ten dollars. The whole tract would not sell for even over a third of a cent an acre now, but some day people will be glad to get it for twenty dollars, fifty dollars, a hundred dollars an acre. (Here he dropped his voice to a whisper and looked anxiously around to see that there were no eavesdroppers—a thousand dollars an acre!)

"Well, you may open your eyes and stare, but it's so. You and I may not see the day, but they'll see it. Nancy, you have heard of steamboats, and maybe you believed in t h e m—of course you did. You have heard these cattle here scoff at them and call them lies and humbugs; they are a reality, and they're going to be a more wonderful thing some day than they are now. They are going to make a revolution in this world's affairs that will make a man dizzy to contemplate. I've been watching—I've been watching while some people slept and I know what's coming. Even you and I will see the day that steamboats will come up that little Turkey River to within twenty miles of this land of ours, and in high water they will come right to it! And this is not all, Nancy; it isn't even half! There's a bigger wonder—the railroad? These worms here have never even heard of it—and when they do they'll not believe in it. But it's another fact. Coaches that fly over the ground twenty miles an hour. It makes a man's brain whirl. Some day, when we are in our graves, there will be a railroad stretching hundreds of miles all the way down from the cities of the northern states to New Orleans—and it's got to run within thirty miles of this land—maybe even through a corner of it. Well, do you know they've quit burning wood in some of the eastern states, and what do you suppose they burn? Coal! (He bent over and whispered again.) There's whole worlds of it on this land. You know that black stuff that crops out on the bank of the branch? Well, that's it. You have taken it for rocks. So has everybody here.* * * One man was going to build a chimney out of it, Nancy. I expect I turned as white as a sheet. Why it might have caught fire and told everything. I showed him it was too crumbly. Then he was going to build it of copper ore—splendid yellow forty per cent ore. There's fortunes upon fortunes upon our land. It scared me to death. The idea of this fool starting a smelting furnace in his house without knowing it and getting dull eyes opened. And then he was going to build it of iron ore! There's mountains of iron here, Nancy, whole mountains of it. I wouldn't take any chance, I just stuck by him—I haunted him —I never let him alone until he built it of mud and sticks, like all the rest of the chimneys in this dismal country.

"Pine forests, wheat land, corn land, iron, copper, coal—wait till the railroads come, and the steamboats!

"We'll never see the day, Nancy, never in the world—never, never, never, child. We's got to drag along, drag along and eat crusts in toil and poverty, all hopeless and forlorn, but they'll ride in coaches, Nancy; they'll live the princes of the earth; they'll be courted and worshipped; their names will be known from ocean to ocean.

BLEDSOE HOUSE, JAMESTOWN

FENTRESS COUNTY HIGH SCHOOL

YELLOW CREEK FALLS

"Ah! well-a-day, will they ever come back here on the steamboat and say: 'This, our little spot, shall not be touched, this hovel shall be saved, for here our father and our mother suffered for us, thought for us, laid the foundation of our future as solid as the hills.' * * * *

"I have a letter from Beriah Sellers—just came this day—I'll read you a line from it. * * * *

"'Come right along to Missouri. Don't wait and worry about a good price, but sell out for whatever you can get, and come along or you might be too late. Throw away your traps if necessary and come empty handed. You'll never regret it. It's the grandest country—the loveliest land—the purest atmosphere—I can't describe it; no pen can do it justice, and its filling up every day—people coming from everywhere. I've got the biggest scheme on earth, and I'll take you in, and I'll take in every friend I've got that's ever stood by me, for there's enough for all, and to spare. Mum's the word—don't whisper —keep yourself to yourself! You'll see. Come, rush—hurry —don't wait for anything.'" * * * *

And with an activity and a suddenness that bewildered Obedstown, and almost took away its breath, the Hawkins' hurried through with their arrangements in four short months and flitted out into the great mysterious blank that lay beyond the knobs of Tennessee.

(The above chapter is copied from the "Gilded Age", by permission of Harper Bros. & Co., New York City, the publishers of the complete work of Mark Twain in twenty-five volumes.

The Si Hawkins referred to in this chapter is said to have been John M. Clemons, the father of Mark Twain. Clemons entered and obtained grants for nearly all the lands in Fentress County in the 30's. He was the first Circuit Court Clerk in Fentress County. Also a practicing attorney at Jamestown. The Turkey River was Obeds River, and Obedstown, Jamestown.

CHAPTER VI

FENTRESS COUNTY IN WAR.
FOURTH TENNESSEE CAVALRY.

THE history which follows is intended to give the important movements in the Civil War in which Bledsoe's Company participated. Much of the time they fought under General Joe Wheeler, and a history of Wheeler's raids is also a history of the part Fentress County played in the Confederate service. It also necessarily shows the battles in which the regiment composed of soldiers from Fentress, Marshall, Sullivan, Smith, Wilson, DeKalb, Cannon, Rutherford, Hamilton, Sumner, Davidson and Knox counties were engaged.

Much of the information was gathered from Maj. George B. Guild's history of the Fourth Tennessee Cavalry Regiment. Some has been picked up from old citizens and soldiers in Fentress and adjoining counties, and from records in the State Capitol.

Commissioned Officers Fourth Tennessee Cavalry, 1862—Colonel, Baxter Smith; Lieut. Colonel, Paul F. Anderson; Major, W. Scott Bledsoe; Adjutant, J. A. Minnis; Sergeant Major, W. A. Rushing; Quartermaster, Marcellus Grissim, with assistants R. O. McLean, Bob Corder and John Price; Captain Bone Commissary, with Lieut. J. A. Arnold and Captain McLean, assistants; Surgeon, Dr. W. T. Delaney; Assistant Surgeon, Dr. Tom Allen; Chaplain, Rev. W. W. Hendricks; Ord. Officer, Finney; Buglers, J. A. Stewart, James B. Nance; Wagon Masters, Bob Gann, Bennett Chapman.

After the battle of Fayetteville, N. C., 1864, Major Scott Bledsoe, of Jamestown, Fentress County, was placed in command of the regiment and Eb Crozier became adjutant of the regiment.

Officers Company "I", Nolensville, Tenn., 1862 — Captain, Bob Bledsoe; Lieutenants, William Hildreth, John W. Story, Foster Bowman and Elliott.

THE OLD HOME OF MARK TWAIN'S ANCESTORS. 19

Recruited at Jamestown, in Fentress County, in 1861.

This company became Company "I" of the Fourth Tennessee Cavalry at Nolensville, Tenn., October, 1862. Was, after this time, under Joe Wheeler. Up to this time the Bledsoe Company was with General Bragg in his Kentucky campaigns. Scott Bledsoe, during this campaign, was captain of the company. Col. Baxter Smith commanded the regiment to which they belonged.

Company "I" killed in battle—Fentress Atkins, at McMinnville, Tenn., 1862; Cullom Jewett, at McMinnville, 1862; Jas. Padgett, Fort Donaldson, 1863; Elias Owens, New Hope Church, Ga., 1864; Capt. Robert Bledsoe, Sparta, Tenn.—Wheeler's raid—1863; A. Bledsoe, Sparta, Tenn.—Wheeler's raid—1863; Lieut. Foster Bowman, Sparta, Tenn.—Wheeler's raid — 1863; Acting Adjutant Eb Crozier, killed on return home in 1865 in East Tennessee; William Beason, Pleasant Poor, John Smith, Mike Hill, Lafayette Hill, Robert Brown, were killed during Wheeler's raid in 1863. Steve Richardson was killed while on a visit home in early part of the war. Fayette Allen was killed at the Dr. Hale place on Wolf River in 1862. W. Allen, W. F. Cummings, J. J. Linder and John Poor are reported as killed in action, on Confederate records in the office of State Pension Board.

Wounded in Company "I" (partial list)—Lieut. J. W. Story, at McMinnville and at New Hope Church, Ga.; B. Porter Harrison, at Fayetteville, N. C., 1865; James Singleton, at New Hope Church, Ga., 1864, had arm amputated; William Beason, wounded in hand a n d side during a visit home in Pickett County.

Survivors of Company "I", 1912—Lieut. John W. Story, Forest City, Ark.; B. P. Harrison, Jamestown, Tenn.; Joel Brown, Glasgow, Ky.; Zack T. Crouch, Bellbuckle, Tenn.; Dr. Henry Signet, Oliver Springs, Tenn.; John Hall, Tennessee; Isaac Ford, Rome, Tenn.; Judge Orville I. Moate, Washington, D. C.; Lieut. W. H. Hildreth, Alvarado, Texas; John N. Simpson, Dallas, Texas; Wm. Wallace, ———, Texas; Jeff Boles, Phoenix, Ariz.; Henry Gatewood, Ennis, Texas.

(This list is taken from Guild's history. It is reported that Wm. H. Hildreth has since died.)

Commissioned officers of companies in Fourth Tenn. Cavalry:

Company A—Captain, D. W. Alexander; First Lieut., Rice McLean; Second Lieut., J. N. Orr; Third Lieut., Chas. Beard. Recruited in Marshall County.

Company B—Captain, C. H. Ingles; First Lieut., Joe Massengale; Second Lieut., Joe Massengale; Third Lieut, G. W. Carmack. Recruited in Sullivan County.

Company C—Captains, Frank Cunningham, George C. Moore; First Lieut., James Hogan; Second Lieut., R. S. Scruggs; Third Lieut., Sam Scoggins. Recruited in Smith County, Tenn.

Company D—Captain, J. M. Phillips; First Lieut., Bob Bone; Second Lieut., J. T. Barbee; Third Lieut., J. A. Arnold. Recruited in DeKalb and Wilson counties.

Company E—Captain, H. A. Wyly; First Lieut., H. L. Preston; Second Lieut., W. S. Sullivan; Third Lieut., John Fathera. Recruited in Cannon County.

Company F—Capt. J. R. Lester; First Lieut., C. S. Burgess; Second Lieut., W. H. Phillips; Third Lieut., James Williamson. Recruited in Wilson County.

Company G—Captain, J. W. Nichol; First Lieut., Dave Youree; Second Lieut., ——— McKnight; Third Lieut., J. A. Sagely. Recruited in Cannon and Rutherford counties.

Company H—Captain, Sam Glover; Lieuts., Green Light, William Gaut and William Fields. Recruited in Hamilton County and Bridgeport, Ala.

Company I—Fentress County; given elsewhere.

Company K—Captain, James Britton; Lieuts., W. Corbett and Dewitt Anderson. Recruited in Wilson, Sumner and Davidson counties.

Company L—Captain, J. J. Parton; Lieuts., Henry, Russell and Tillery. Recruited in Knox County.

CHAPTER VII

BLEDSOE'S COMPANY FROM 1861 to OCT., 1862.

THIS company of Confederate cavalry was made up in Fentress County at the beginning of the war. In August, 1861, the Twenty-eighth Tennessee Confederate Regiment was formed at Camp Zollicoffer, in Overton County. This regiment was at first commanded by Col. John P. Murray, who was soon afterward elected to the Confederate Congress, and S. S. Stanton succeeded him as commander of the regiment. Other officers of the regiment were Lieut. Col. John Eatherly, Major James H. Talburt, Dr. Clay, Surgeon; Dr. Eli Hawthorne, Assistant Surgeon; Joshua Hale, Asst. Q. M. and J. B. Anderson, Asst. Com.

The regiment was made up of companies from White, Wilson, Putnam, Jackson and Smith. This regiment, with the Twenty-fifth Tennessee, Capt. Nat Sanders' company of cavalry, and Capt. W. Scott Bledsoe's cavalry, was ordered to report to Albert Sidney Johnson, at Bowling Green, Ky. In obedience to this order they marched from Camp Zollicoffer to Bowling Green. Finally they were attached to General Bragg's army and served under him in his Kentucky campaign, Col. Baxter Smith commanding the regiment to which they belonged. They took part in the battle of Munfordville, Ky., Murfreesboro, Tenn. (June, 1862), and at Mill Springs, Ky., Bardstown, and at Perryville, October 8, 1862.

CHAPTER VIII

IN October, 1862, Bledsoe's company became a part of the Fourth Tennessee Cavalry Regiment, under Col. Baxter Smith, and was called Company "I", being reorganized at Nolensville, Tenn. This regiment was made up at first of ten companies, designated as companies A, B, C, D, E, F, G, H, I and K. These were all recruited in Middle Tennessee, except Company B, which was recruited in Sullivan County, and Company H, recruited in Hamilton County and northern Alabama, at Bridgeport. Company L, from Knox County, was attached to the regiment just before the battle of Chickamauga. This regiment, with the Eighth Texas, Eleventh Texas, First Kentucky and Malone's Battalion (Alabama), formed a brigade. Col. Tom Harrison, as Senior Colonel, commanded the brigade, Maj. Gen. John A. Wharton commanding the division. (Gen. Joe Wheeler's Corps, Army of Tennessee.)

Their first service under this organization was at Franklin, Tenn., on outpost duty, Gen. Rosecrans at that time holding Nashville for the Union.

From October, 1862, to January, 1863, this company, with the regiment, remained a few miles from Nashville, watching Rosecrans and preventing, as much as possible, Rosecrans' army from leaving Nashville and from foraging upon the country.

Several engagements were had with portions of Rosecrans' command. Men were constantly being lost upon each side.

Finally, Rosecrans attacked the Confederate forces at Murfreesboro. Several thousand were lost to each side in this battle in killed, wounded and captured, but it is generally conceded that the Confederates had the victory won if Bragg had kept up the fight, but a few days of inactivity on his part gave the Union army a chance to collect their forces and fortify themselves on a knoll on Stones River. Here the Confederates attacked and were repulsed and Bragg retreated to Shelbyville. According to the records I have before me Fentress Adkins and Cullom Jewett were the only soldiers in Company "I" to be killed in 1862. They are both reported to have been killed at McMinnville, Tenn.

J. F., or Fentress, Adkins had served as a soldier in the Mexican War and was a brave soldier, as his comrades knew him. His widow, Nancy (Choate) Adkins, died a few years ago. His son, Dud Adkins, who has served as constable and as Justice of the Peace of his district, lives near Glenobey, in Fentress County, Tenn. Two other sons, Thomas and Francis Adkins, are still living, Francis in the west and Thomas in Cumberland County, Tenn.

After Bragg retreated to Shelbyville the Fourth Tennessee, under Wheeler, was sent to Ft. Donelson to try to retake it. Wheeler made an unsuccessful attempt to do so and lost a number of men. Among them was James Padgett, of Bledsoe's company. This was in January, 1863.

The Fourth Tennessee then returned to Shelbyville. The regiment was then detached and sent to Woodbury to relieve a portion of General Morgan's command under Captain Hutchinson, who was killed here. (One Capt. Hutchinson was killed in a skirmish with Tinker Beaty's company, near the Katy Boles place in what is now Pickett County, or at least it is so understood by everybody in this section. Guild's history gives it as stated above.)

The Federals at this time camped at Murfreesboro, and the Fourth Tennessee had several engagements with parts of that command. After some weeks they were sent to Trousdale's Ferry on Caney Fork, and from there to Edgefield Junction, where a train load of horses was captured and the train destroyed.

Some Federal officers and men were captured by them at Smyrna and paroled. Soon afterward the regiment returned to Tullahoma. They then crossed the Cumberland Mountains to near Chattanooga, and on to Rome, Ga., where they remained for about two months, feeding and resting their horses as well as themselves. After doing duty for a short time in and around Chattanooga, they participated in the battle of Chickamauga, September 19 and 20, 1863. Rosecrans commanded the Federal army and Bragg the Confederates. The Fourth Tennessee took a prominent part in this battle, losing about forty men in the engagement.

CHAPTER IX

WHEELER'S RAID, 1863.

IMMEDIATELY after the battle of Chickamauga, Bragg ordered Wheeler into Tennessee to cut off all supplies from Rosecrans, who was then in possession of Chattanooga. They forded the Tennessee River at Cottonport, about thirty miles above Chattanooga, the Fourth Tennessee leading the way. This regiment was fired upon just as they reached the north bank of the river by a small body of men. The fire was returned and the attacking party disappeared. The command continued on to the Sequatchie Valley. Here they found seven hundred and fifty wagons loaded with supplies for Rosecrans. These were guarded by about twelve hundred men, who were captured after a short resistance. They also captured about twenty-six hundred mules. The wagons were loaded principally with provision which had loaded at McMinnville, then in charge of the Federal army. Rosecrans fearing to try to bring them further on the train had his supplies unloaded there and sent through by heavily guarded wagons. Everything was destroyed that could not be taken along by a cavalry force. The wreckage included wagons, mules, harness and provisions, and it is said covered acres of ground.

They went from here with their prisoners to McMinnville, which Dibrell had already retaken, capturing 400 Federals. Dibrell had also captured an immense amount of clothing and stores intended for shipment to Rosecrans at Chattanooga.

The sixteen hundred soldiers captured by Wheeler and Dibrell were paroled and started toward Kentucky. Wheeler's mission to cut off supplies from Rosecrans did not afford an opportunity to hold prisoners, so the best he could do was to parole them and let them go.

From McMinnville they went to Murfreesboro, tearing up several miles of railroad. One hundred Federals were captured and paroled at Christiana. They then went to Pulaski by way of Shelbyville. On their way they encountered a Federal force at Farmington. Here the Fourth Tennessee, under Maj. Paul Anderson, and the First Kentucky, u n d e r Col. Cheneyworth, were cut off from the regular command. They forced their way through with the loss of only a few men. John P. Hickman, Secretary of t h e present State Pension Board, was captured here and held a prisoner till the close of the war.

At Richland Creek, near Pulaski, the Fourth Tennessee was detailed to hold the bridge across that creek until sundown, so as to prevent the Federals from pursuing. Here they watched and waited for sundown, expecting to be fired upon every minute. However, the Federals did not pursue them. Shortly after the sun disappeared for the day they followed their command, overtaking them the next day. They crossed the Tennessee near Bainbridge, Alabama. Only about four weeks before they had crossed the river at Cottonport and started on this celebrated raid. During this raid Wheeler killed, wounded and captured three thousand men, burned and brought out one thousand wagons, captured thirty-five hundred horses and mules, half of which they lost in the fight at Farmington. They also destroyed many miles of railroad then in possession of the Federals and much clothing and provisions that would have reached Rosecrans.

This raid began about the last of September and ended in October, 1863. From the information gathered it appears that nine of Bledsoe's company lost their lives during the raid. Captain R. H. Bledsoe, Lieut. Foster Bowman and A. Bledsoe were killed at Sparta; Pleasant Poor on Mill Creek in Overton County; William Beason, John Smith, Mike Hill, Fayette Hill, Robert Brown, W. Allen, J. J. Linder, John Poor and W. F. Cummings are reported on Confederate records and from other sources as having been killed in action, but the author has not been able to locate where each was killed.

CHAPTER X

FOURTH TENNESSEE IN GEORGIA.

WHEN Sherman began his march from Chattanooga to Atlanta he met his first resistance from the Fourth Tennessee, who were holding a position at Tunnel Hill, Ga., a short distance below Chattanooga. From here to Atlanta fighting continued more or less every day, in all of which this regiment took part. George B. Guild, in his history, says: "The distance from Dalton to Atlanta is about seventy-five miles. The contending armies were seventy-five days in covering the distance—a little over a mile a day. It was a great battle scene from its beginning to its close. At night the camp fires of the two armies were visible one from the other. A number of large battles were fought, and many were killed and wounded on both sides. The daytime was an incessant crash of musketry from the skirmishers and heavy cannonading from batteries. In fact from the number killed and wounded in many of these skirmishes they would be called battles at the present time." * * * *

After the fall of Atlanta, July 27, 1864, Wheeler, with the Fourth Tennessee Cavalry as part of his corps, was ordered by Hood to go below Atlanta to intercept the commands of McCook and Stoneman respectively, who had been sent by Sherman to release the Federal prisoners at Andersonville, Ga., and to capture stores, etc., on their way. Wheeler sent Gen. Dibrell after Stoneman, and with his own command he followed McCook, overtaking him at Jonesboro. After some fighting he retreated to Newnan, followed by Wheeler. After a battle lasting about two hours McCook, with fifteen hundred soldiers, surrendered.

Gen. Dibrell was also successful in capturing Stoneman.

Soon after these successes, Wheeler's corps rendezvoused at Covington, Ga., for a few days, and was then ordered back to Tennessee. He came by way of Dalton to Strawberry Plains, near Knoxville, where they met and defeated a Federal cavalry force, driving them back into Knoxville with the loss of a few men.

From Knoxville they again went into the Sequatchie valley, where the Fourth Tennessee Cavalry was detached and sent to Tracy City for the purpose of capturing a force at that place, who were said to be occupying an unfinished fort. An unsuccessful attempt was made to take the place, but it proved too strong for the attacking force. Lieut. W. H. Phillips was severely wounded. Several other Confederates were also wounded.

From Tracy City the Fourth went to Lebanon to again join Wheeler. As most of this regiment necessarily passed near their homes, "many of them were allowed to visit their homes to remount themselves, pick up absentees and obtain recruits if possible." Several of Bledsoe's company were killed while on visits home. Among them were Pleasant and John Poor, Fayette Allen and Steve Richardson. Pleasant Poor was killed on Mill Creek in Overton County, Fayette Allen was killed at the Dr. Hale place on Wolf River, Steve Richardson was killed near Chanute.

CHAPTER XI

SALTVILLE, VIRGINIA.

THE next engagement in which the Fourth Tennessee participated was probably Woodbury, where some of them were killed, some wounded and a few taken prisoners. Next they went to Sparta, and from there, by way of Crossville, to Saltville, Virginia. Here they encountered some negro Federal soldiers, the first they had met. About six hundred men are said to have been killed on each side. Breckenridge was the Confederate and Burbridge the Federal commander. Each side had about three thousand men. Burbridge made an unsuccessful attempt to take possession of the salt works at this place. Much of East Tennessee and eastern Kentucky depended upon this place for salt supply.

General Guild says of this battle: "That night we pursued the enemy, passing over the mountains to a gap with the view of cutting them off. They had to travel over a distance of forty miles on a well built macadamized road. The mountain path to the gap was only twelve miles in length, and the men had to dismount and lead their horses.

"The night was very dark and it was hard to discern the path. Occasionally a horse would make a misstep and tumble down the steep mountain side. You could hear the noise of falling stones for minutes afterwards as they rolled down and down the precipitous mountain side. We were told afterwards by some of these soldiers, that they found their horses miles below where they fell. I have occasionally met an old soldier who was at Saltville, and about the first thing he would say would be: 'Did you ever experience anything like that dark night ride at Saltville, Virginia?' And the wonder is that a number of men were not dashed to pieces down the steep slope below. We reached the gap at daylight. Burbridge's rear guard was passing through and we killed and wounded a few of them.

GENERAL WILLIAMS.

"When General Williams left Sparta for the Army of Tennessee at Atlanta all of the independents and bushwhackers in that part of the State went out with him. It got so hot thereabout, and the Federals were swarming so in Tennessee (like bees), that they concluded the better part of valor was to get away. Champ Ferguson on the one side and David Beaty on the other, both I believe from Fentress County, were the respective leaders. A warfare had been raging in this part of the State and in southern Kentucky since the beginning of the war.

"Champ Ferguson and his followers participated actively at Saltville. After the battle was over a Lieutenant Smith of the Federal army was left with others wounded. He was taken to Emory and Henry College, which was made a hospital for both armies. When Ferguson heard the fact, he went over and killed Lieutenant Smith. It was said that during the war Smith had killed a Colonel Hamilton, who was a comrade, neighbor and personal friend of Ferguson; that Smith had captured Hamilton after a fight between members of the two clans and had been ordered, with a squad of soldiers, to take him to headquarters over in Kentucky; but that after starting with his prisoner, and going a short distance, he ordered his men to take Hamilton to the side of the public road, where he was stood up by a tree and shot to death."

FERGUSON EXECUTED.

General Guild, continuing, says: "A short time after the Confederates had returned from the surrender, in May, 1865, Ferguson, who had surrendered to the Federals, was undergoing trial by court martial at Nashville.

"He had been arrested at Saltville, Virginia, by order of General Williams, the Confederate commander, for the alleged killing of Smith and sent to Richmond, as we understood it, and we saw him no more afterwards. The war terminated a short time after this. I presume, in the confusion of things, he was permitted to return to his home in Tennessee. I was told that frequent attempts had been made to capture him, but finally, after being advised, and on being assured by Federal authority that if he would surrender he would be given the same terms that had been extended to other Confederates, he gave up. After this he was placed on trial by a military court martial at Nashville to answer various charges of murder. Among them was the charge of the murder of Lieutenant Smith, at Emory and Henry College in Virginia. He was convicted and executed by hanging at Nashville."

Champ Ferguson was in jail at Jamestown when the war came up, awaiting trial on the charge of murder. Both he and his victim had lived near Chanute, in what was then Fentress County, now Pickett. When the war broke out he was released and was never tried for this offense.

CHAPTER XII

SHERMAN'S MARCH TO THE SEA, NOV. 15, 1864.

SHERMAN was about five weeks in the celebrated march from Atlanta to Savannah. The Fourth Tennessee Cavalry, under Wheeler, followed him in obedience to orders from General Hood. They were engaged with a part of Sherman's army at Macon, also at Waynesboro. Several were killed in these engagements. At Buckhead Church, Wheeler attacked Kilpatrick's Cavalry, losing several men and more horses than in any other battle of the war.

After Sherman had taken Savannah, and began his march through South Carolina and North Carolina, Wheeler's command followed and did what it could to prevent Sherman from destroying the property along the line of march.

On February 16, 1865, a battle was fought near Fayetteville, N. C., known as the Kilpatrick fight. (Kilpatrick was the Federal commander.) Several were killed and wounded on each side. Among them were Lieut. Paul Anderson, of the Fourth Tennessee. B. P. Harrison, of Company I, was also wounded. Lieut. Massengale, of Co. B, was among the killed.

After this battle Major Scott Bledsoe became the commander of the Fourth Tennessee, succeeding Paul Anderson, who was severely wounded. Lieut. Eb Crozier was made adjutant of the regiment.

BENTONVILLE, NORTH CAROLINA.

The battle of Bentonville was fought on March 20, 1865. The Fourth Tennessee was ordered forward at the opening of this engagement. They were fired upon by Sherman's men and returned the fire. Several of the regiment fell before they received orders to fall back. In this battle it is said that the Fourth Tennessee and the Eighth Texas saved Johnson's army from capture by a successful charge upon the Federals, driving them back several hundred yards from a bridge that spanned Mill Creek, and kept them back some time, thus making it possible for the Confederate army to cross the bridge and escape.

CHAPTER XIII

THE SURRENDER.

THE Fourth Tennessee, which at first had about eleven hundred men, at its surrender at Charlotte, N. C., on May 3, 1865, had only two hundred and fifty men. More than half of these were battle-scarred. Many of them had been wounded more than once and in different engagements.

When the news came that the Confederates were to surrender, the Third Arkansas and the Eighth and the Eleventh Texas left the brigade for the West, where they intended to join another command for the purpose of further fighting.

While the news was being circulated that an armistice had been agreed upon, pending arrangements to allow all to return to their homes, the sad news came one night that Lincoln had been assassinated and that the armistice was over. The Fourth was ordered to Rufin's Bridge to guard the road to Raleigh. Silently, it is said, they moved to their post of duty. After placing their pickets for the night, a courier came with the news that another armistice had been agreed upon. So again they went to their camp and were never again called to do duty in the field. In a short time they received their discharges and were soon on their way homeward. The infantry were discharged at Greensboro, North Carolina, t h e cavalry at Charlotte.

GENERAL WHEELER'S FAREWELL ADDRESS.

Headquarters Cavalry Corps, April 28, 1865.

Gallant Comrades:

You have fought your fight, your task is done. During a four years fight for liberty you have exhibited courage, fortitude and devotion. You are the victors of more than two hundred strongly contested fields; you have participated in more than a thousand conflicts of arms; you are heroes, victors and patriots. The bones of your comrades mark the battlefields upon the soil of Kentucky, Tennessee, North Carolina, South Carolina, Georgia, Alabama, Mississippi and Virginia.

You have done all that human exertion could accomplish. In bidding you adieu, I desire to tender to you my thanks for your gallantry in battle and your devotion at all times to the holy cause you have done so much to maintain. I desire also to express my gratitude for the kind feelings you have seen fit to extend towards myself, and to evoke upon you the blessings of your heavenly father, to whom we must always look for support in the hour of distress.

JOE WHEELER, *Major General.*

CHAPTER XIV

MAJOR SCOTT BLEDSOE.

WHEN the war broke out, Scott Bledsoe was practicing law at Jamestown. He and his brothers were all prominent as well as their father, Wm. M. Bledsoe. They held various official positions in the county before the war. The old house in which the Bledsoe's lived is still standing. This family is related to the Bledsoe's of Sumner County.

Bates Bledsoe was killed in the Mexican War, and Captains R. H. and A. Bledsoe were killed at Sparta during one of Wheeler's raids, in which they were participating. Scott made up a cavalry company at Jamestown early in 1861 and was elected captain. Later he became a major. He took part in all the engagements in which the Fourth Tennessee Cavalry took part, and received his discharge at Charlotte, N. C., May 3, 1865.

Scott Bledsoe died at Cleburne, Texas, a few years ago a highly respected and well-to-do citizen.

Very few of this company ever returned to Fentress County to make their homes after the war, owing to the local warfare that existed for some years. The feeling was very bitter in this county between the Confederate and Union sympathizers, the Union side being greatly in the majority.

At present all evidences of the old feeling is entirely gone, and members of Bledsoe's company, on recent visits to the county, have found their old enemies among those who made them feel welcome back in their native county.

One of the survivors, B. Porter Harrison, has spent most of his time for several years at Jamestown with his son, G. E. Harrison, and his daughter, Mrs. E. M. Shelley.

Robert H. Bledsoe succeeded his brother as captain of the company at Nolensville, Tennessee, in October, 1862, when the regiment was reorganized, and served in this capacity until he was killed at Sparta the next year.

COMPANY D, EIGHTH TENNESSEE VOLUNTEERS.

In addition to those who served in the Confederate army under Bledsoe, several enlisted in other commands. Among them were the following who served in Capt. Calvin E. Myer's company, known as Company D of Eighth Tennessee:

Robt. Boles, Third Sergt.; Van Huddleston, Dode Stephens, Miles, Nick and Elijah Stephens, and Hilery and Peyton Smith.

(There were probably others in this company from Fentress, these are all I could find.)

Nick, Miles and Elijah Stephens and Peyton Smith were reported as killed in battle. Dode Stephens was killed while at home near the close of the war. His widow, "Aunt" Sally Stephens, lived on Indian Creek, and drew a State pension until her death in 1913 at the age of about one hundred.

Company D took part in the following battles: Cheat Mountain, Va., Port Royal, S. C., Corinth, Miss., Perryville, Ky., Murfreesboro, Chickamauga, Missionary Ridge and Kings Mountain, near Dalton, Ga.; Resaca, New Hope Church, Burnt Corner, Powder Springs, Marietta, Atlanta, Eastport and Jonesboro, Ga., Franklin, Tenn., and Nashville, and surrendered at Asheville, N. C., in 1865.

CAPTAIN CALVIN E. MYERS.

Capt. Myers of Company D, Eighth Tennessee, resides at Livingston. He was a soldier in the Mexican War, and was a comrade of J. F. Adkins and the Bledsoes and the other Fentress countainians in this war. He is one of the few survivors of the war.

Sergeant Robert Boles lived at the Andy Garrett place south of Jamestown when the war came up. His widow now lives on Spring Creek in Overton County.

CHAPTER XV

UNION COMMANDS AND COMMANDERS.
CAPTAIN MITCHELL R. MILLSAPS.

CAPTAIN MILLSAPS was a native of Fentress, being a son of Hiram and Marsha Millsaps. On the 10th day of August, 1861, he was made captain of a company of infantry for the U. S. A., which he recruited in Fentress County. His company became a part of the Second Tennessee Infantry. After serving until November, 1863, they were captured at Rogersville. An account of their services appears elsewhere.

He resided in the Poplar Cove and followed farming and logging until his death several years ago.

CAPTAIN TINKER DAVID BEATY.

David Beaty, known as Tinker, was a native of Fentress County, and a son of George Beaty, who came from North Carolina with his brothers, John and David Beaty, in pioneer days, and settled on the East Fork, George Beaty settling what is now known as the Richard Smith place. Here David was born in 1823, and lived near the old home all his life and died in 1883.

He formed a company early in the Civil War, known as David Beaty's Independent Scouts and was made captain. Their purpose was to protect the mountain country from invasion by the Confederates. The author is indebted to C. Beaty, son of Tinker Beaty, for the information in regard to skirmishes herein described.

Tinker Beaty's Company—In 1861 they had a skirmish with Bledsoe's men, near the Albertson schoolhouse. Lieutenant Riddle, who lives near Monterey, and another man was wounded. The next engagement was near Glenoby, also near the home of Captain Beaty. Two or three were wounded in this engagement.

This company met and defeated a Confederate force of fifty or sixty men at the Wash Taylor stand, nine miles south of Jamestown, about 1862. Two wagon loads of drugs and paper for striking Confederate money were being smuggled through from Kentucky with the intention of taking it to the Confederate government. The Confederates were forced to run off and leave the plunder in the hands of the attacking company. A man named Baldwin was seriously wounded.

In 1863 they fought a battle with some Confederates under Captain Hutchinson, near the George Boles place, in what is now Pickett County. Captain Hutchinson was killed and two or three others wounded. Among them was W. E. Linder, who was with Hutchinson. He was shot, a minnie ball passing through his body. Although the wound was a very dangerous one, he still survives, and lives near Poteet, Tennessee.

Another skirmish took place near Van Buren Academy in Poplar Cove. The Confederate lieutenant, Wm. Goggins, was killed and a few others wounded.

In 1864, Beaty's company attacked Col. Hughes' company, which had come up from the lower counties into Fentress on a foraging expedition. This fight occurred in the Buffalo Cove. Thomas Culver and Jop Moody of Tinker's company were killed and several Confederates wounded.

This company was engaged in many other skirmishes in Fentress, Overton, Clay, Pickett, Cumberland and White counties in Tennessee, and in southern Kentucky.

After the war was over Champ Ferguson came to Jamestown and attempted the arrest of Capt. Beaty. Beaty mounted a race horse and ran off and left him, receiving three wounds, from which he soon recovered. He was a leader in Fentress during reconstruction days and until his death in 1883. He was a very clever, hospitable man among his neighbors and was generally liked by them.

CAPTAIN RUFUS DOWDY.

Rufus Dowdy lived on Wolf River at the breaking out of the war. He was forty-three years old at the opening of the war. He assisted in recruiting a company for the Union service. It became Company D of Eleventh Tennessee. He was made lieutenant December 4, 1863, and captain February 20, 1864. The roster of officers and men appears elsewhere.

His son, O. P. Dowdy, resides now in Pickett County.

At first he was captain of a company known as the Home Guards. Their principal service in this capacity was in opposing Confederate forces entering their territory.

CHAPTER XVI

THE SECOND EAST TENN. VOL. INF.

THIS regiment was recruited at Camp Dick Robinson in Kentucky, September 28, 1861, and left there October 18, 1861; fought the Confederates at Wildcat, Ky., London, Somerset and at Mill Springs. Left Mill Springs January 21, 1862, and marched to Cumberland Ford, Ky. On the 7th of March they left Cumberland Ford and marched across the mountains via Boston, Ky., to Big Creek Gap, where they routed and captured a Confederate force under the command of Lieut. Col. J. F. White, destroyed a large amount of quartermaster and commissary stores, captured eighty-nine horses and mules and a large amount of small arms, ammunition, etc. Remained at Cumberland Ford till the first of June, 1862, then marched back to Cumberland Gap, reaching there June 18th, and remained there till September 17th, when the Federal forces, under George W. Morgan, evacuated the gap and marched through the eastern part of Kentucky to the Ohio River, then through southern Ohio to Saline Salt Works in Kanawha Valley, W. Va. Left there November, 1862, and marched to Point Pleasant on the Ohio River; then they went by water to Louisville, Ky. From Louisville they went by land to Murfreesboro and took part in this battle. Remained at Murfreesboro till March 10, 1863, then returned to Kentucky for the purpose of being mounted, which was done about the first of June, 1863. Remained in Kentucky and participated in divers engagements with the Confederate forces under Pegram, Scott and others, until the Fourth of July, when they left Somerset in pursuit of the Confederate, General Morgan, in his raid through Kentucky, Indiana and Ohio. Was present at Salineville, W. Va., when Morgan was captured. Returned to Kentucky by way of Cincinnati, joining General Burnside's forces at Stamford, Ky., for the East Tennessee campaign. Led the advance forces at Wolf Creek and at Loudon. Went from Loudon to Knoxville, and to Cumberland Gap, where they de-

THE OLD HOME OF MARK TWAIN'S ANCESTORS. 41

feated the Confederate forces under General Phrasier. Returned then to Knoxville and took the advance of the column that moved into upper East Tennessee. This regiment brought on and participated in the battle of Blue Springs, pursued the retreating Confederate forces under Gens. Jones, Williams and Jackson until it drove their pickets in at Abingdon, Va.; destroyed a large amount of stores, etc.; also destroyed the railroads about Bristol; returned to Rogersville, where the regiment was captured on the 6th of November, 1863, by the forces under the Confederate General Jones.

A few of the regiment escaped and reported at Knoxville, taking part in the siege. All that was left of the whole regiment (106) was mustered out at Knoxville October 6, 1864.

Officers and enlisted men, Fentress and adjoining counties, 1861 to 1865. (Partial list) U. S. Army:

Capt. John C. Wright, Co. D, 11th Tenn. Cav. Reg.
Lieut. Lemuel C. Wright, Co. D, 2d Tenn.
Lieut. David F. Huddleston, Co. D, 2d Tenn.
Lieut. J. W. Gaudin, 11th Tenn. Cav., later became Q. M. of Reg.
Lieut. Elias Carroll, Co. B.
Lieut. Wm. Stone, Co. D.
Capt. Wiley C. Huddleston, 11th Tenn. Cav.
Lieut. Wm. H. Williams, Co. H, 10th Cav.
Chap. Sam Greer, 11th Tenn. Cav. Reg.
Lieut. Joseph S. Chatman, Co. A, 11th Tenn. Cav.
Lieut. Wm. J. Norrod, Co. D, 1st Tenn. Mtd. Inf.
Lieut. Elijah Garrett, 1st Tenn. Mtd. Inf.
Lieut. Wm. A. Overstreet, Co. A, 11th Tenn. Cav.
Maj. Abraham E. Garrett, 1st Tenn. Mtd. Inf., Pro. Lieut. Col. 3/20/64.
Capt. Wade Jones, Co. C.
James W. Wright, Sergt. Maj. 1st Regt. Mtd. Inf.

OFFICERS 1ST. REGT. MTD. INFT.

Lieut. Col. A. E. Garrett, Pro. Lieut. Col. 3/18/64, Maj. 6/28/64.
Maj. Francis M. McKee, Pro. 8/19/64.
1st Lieut. and Adjt. L. P. Martin, 3/24/64.
1st Lieut. and R. Q. M. Luke P. Gillem, 1/31/64.
Surg. Chas. C. Shoyer, 3/7/64.
Surg. Lem. A. Robeson, 2/19/64.
Surg. Chris. C. Clements, 4/16/64.
Sergt. Maj. Jas. W. Wright, 9/25/63.
Com. Ser. James S. Palmer, 10/21/63.
Hosp. Steward Joseph A. Pendarvis, 1/21/64.

ROLL CO. D, 1ST TENN. MTD. INF.
(Copied from Military Records.)
Officers.

Name	Age	Enlisted	Promoted
Capt. Rufus Dowdy	43		12/ 4/63
1st Lieut Lem C. Wright	26	9/10/63 in this Co	2/20/64
2d Lieut. Wm. J. Norred	26	10/10/63	2/20/64
Sergt. Geo. W. Franklin	23	9/ 1/63	2/20/64
Sergt. Joel L. Reagan	22	9/25/63	2/20/64
Sergt. Oliver P. Dowdy	19	1/ 1/64 Cor. 2/20/64.	8/31/64
Sergt. Moses H. Jackson	19	8/20/63	2/20/64
Sergt. James P. Gunnels	21	8/10/63	2/20/64
Corp. Thomas P. Mathews	32	10/10/62	2/20/64
Corp. Joel G. Huddleston	18	1/25/64	2/20/64
Corp. Freeling H. Ogletree	19	8/ 1/63	2/20/64
Corp. James A. Ashburn	23	2/ 8/64	2/20/64
Corp. Anderson Jones	18	1/25/64	2/20/64
Corp. George W. Taber	21	10/10/63	2/20/64
Corp. James A. Hunter	18	2/10/64	8/31/64
Musc. Charles H. Marshall	18	2/12/64	
Musc. James Wright	18	2/12/64	
Corp. Preston B. Robbins	20	2/ 9/64 Killed in Overton County 6/15/64	

Private Soldiers, Co. D.

Name	Age	Enlisted	Mustered in
Franklin Ausbern	27	8/29/63	1/23/64
Sam Bowman	24	8/10/63	1/23/64
William Bowman	27	8/10/63	1/23/64
John H. Burton	42	12/27/63	1/23/64
Thomas Breeding	17	12/26/63	1/23/64
Jas. K. Beaty	20	1/25/64	3/18/64
Andrew J. Beaty	18	1/25/64	3/18/64
Elijah Brummett	30	2/12/64	3/18/64
James Clark	23	1/ 1/64	3/18/64
Isaac Derwese	18	1/ 1/64	1/23/64
Jack Franklin	29	2/25/64	3/18/64
Ambrose M. Grace	19	9/10/63	1/23/64
Jesse Garner	20	12/23/63	1/23/64
Elijah Garrett	18	1/25/64	3/18/64
J. W. Huddleston	22	8/10/63	1/23/64
Wm. E. Huddleston	20	8/10/63	1/23/64
Sandy E. Hicks	21	12/23/63	1/23/64
Thos. Huddleston	34	1/25/64	3/18/64
David Hall	43	1/25/64	3/18/64

THE OLD HOME OF MARK TWAIN'S ANCESTORS. 43

Name	Age	Enlisted	Mustered in
Thomas C. Jackson	20	1/ 3/64	6/23/64
George W. German	20	1/21/64	6/23/64
Sperry C. Jackson	18	2/12/64	3/18/64
Wm. Jones	18	2/12/64	3/18/64
John A. Lewis	19	1/ 3/64	1/23/64
Nathan Mainerd	23	12/31/63	1/23/64
James Mullins	23	8/10/63	1/23/64
Wintan Mullinax	18	1/25/64	3/18/64
Andrew J. Maxfield	22	8/21/63	1/23/64
Alex. Norred	33	10/10/63	1/23/64
Lewis Norred		10/10/63	1/23/64
Benj. Norred	18	10/10/63	1/23/64
Thos. Norris	20	10/10/63	1/23/64
Francis M. Padgett	19	10/10/63	1/23/64
Sam Prior	18	8/19/63	1/23/64
Moses Phillips	27	1/25/64	3/18/64
Geo. W. Polston	19	2/15/64	3/18/64
James Pennycough	18	1/25/64	3/18/64
William Ritch	44	8/10/63	1/23/64
Thomas Reagan, Jr.	18	2/12/64	3/18/64
John Reeder	21	8/12/63	1/23/64
John Smith	18	8/23/63	1/23/64
Henry Stewart	19	12/31/63	1/23/64
Thos. Spyey	20	10/20/63	1/23/64
Francis M. Smith	19	2/10/64	3/18/64
Oliver Spencer	23	1/23/63	3/18/64
Thomas Harrison	18	1/23/63	6/23/64
Thomas Henderson	30	12/18/63	6/23/64
Alex. Whited	26	10/10/63	6/23/64
William Way	18	12/31/63	6/23/64
James Willis	18	12/27/63	6/23/64
Mantin Woolbright	19	12/10/63	6/23/64
Wm. Whited	19	1/ 3/64	6/23/64
Joshua Wright	18	2/12/64	3/18/64
James K. Zachary	18	8/10/63	1/23/64
Chas. C. Burton	45	12/27/63	Killed 4/28/64 at Carthage, accident
Francis M. Derewese	34	12/31/63	Killed 5/7/64 by guerrillas in Smith Co.
William H. Garrett	28	10/10/63	Died 6/2/64 of disease
Thos. McDonald	19	9/15/63	Died 5/30/64 of disease
Geo. H. Owen	18	2/20/64	Captured and killed 6/15/64, Overton Co.
James K. Reagan	18	9/25/63, 1/23/64, Died 10/16/64 of disease	

Name	Age	Enlisted	
Robert White	37	10/10/63,	1/23/64, Killed in action 2/13/64
Joseph Brummett	23	8/10/63	
Thos. Franklin	18	1/25/64	
Andrew J. Fletcher	18	2/12/64	
Daniel Gibson	18	12/23/63	
Jasper Phillips		10/10/63	

ROLL CO. D, 2d TENN.

Name	Age	Enlisted	
Capt. Sam C. Honeycutt	30	9/23/61	
Serg. David H. Walker	52	6/19/62	
Corp. Sam Thompson	18	11/17/61	
John Barger	18	3/10/62	
Jas. M. Beaty	25	12/15/61	
Hubbert Blalock	18	6/10/61	
William Brannon	29	12/15/61	
John K. Brient	18	3/ 9/62	
John Burk		7/16/63	Not mustered in
Wm. E. Brient	16	3/ 9/62	
Pleas M. Burk		7/16/63	Not mustered in
Jas. M. Chilebass		2/11/62	
*Philip Conatser		1/10/62	
Thos. C. Conner	20	1/ 3/62	
Willis W. Cope		1/20/62	
Robt. Dobson		8/15/63	
†Samuel Evans	33	12/15/62	
Hiram Lindley	21	5/11/63	
Andrew J. Garrett		Discharged for disease 8/10/63. Rejected for reinlistment	
Nathan Halbert	21	12/15/61	
Marion Hix	21	12/21/61	
David C. Honeycut	17	3/ 7/62	
Joel G. Huddleston	44	12/15/61	
George W. Jones	36	5/11/63	
Silas Jones		5/11/63	
Jas. W. Keer	19	5/11/63	
Jas. F King	18	5/11/63	
Thomas Knight	18	5/11/63	

†Samuel Evans remained a prisoner at Bells Island for thirteen months, was released and died in the service at Murfreesboro, 1865.

*Philip Conatser of Co. D died in prison at Andersonville, Ga., on March 28, 1864, and was buried in grave No. 216.

Name	Age	Enlisted	
John Looper	34	7/10/62	
Emison Looper	39	7/20/62	
Zach Lord			
Nathaniel Mullinix		12/15/61	
William Mannon		12/ 1/61	
John L. Narramore	20	2/18/63	
James L. Narramore	24	7/16/63	Rejected
Andrew Owen	28	12/15/61	
Robt. Renfree	39	3/ 7/63	
Sol Ringley	22	1/ 3/62	
Wm. H. Ringley	21	2/20/62	
John Ragon		12/15/61	
William Sells	38	12/15/61	
Sam Sells	28	12/15/61	
William Smith	22	1/25/62	
Thos. Stephens	21	5/11/63	
Stephen F. Walker	27	6/ 3/62	
George Walker	18	6/10/62	
Peter Weaver	23	2/24/62	
John Weaver	19	3/30/62	
Pleasant Weaver	21	2/24/62	
Jesse L. Wright	19	5/ 6/63	
Isaac White	18	8/30/63	Not mustered in
Micager York		4/10/63	
John W. Gordon, 2d Lieut.		6/19/63	
Joseph H. Wright		12/15/61	Discharged for disease, 1862
Abner Davidson		12/15/61	Died Jan. 19, 1862
David C. Beaty		12/15/61	Died Feb. 17, 1862
Wm. R. Beaty		12/15/61	Died March 12, 1862
John Gawney		12/15/61	Died June 27, 1862
John Holbert		12/15/61	Died March 16, 1862
Thomas King		7/16/63	Died Feb. 20, 1864
Andrew Poor		3/10/62	Died May 20, 1862
James M. Robbins		12/15/61	Died April 6, 1862
James S. Scarborough			Died March 5, 1863
Tollett Barger		3/10/62	
Alfred Barger		3/10/62	
B. F. Elliot		3/10/62	
John Y. Hix		3/10/62	
Jesse Hix		3/10/62	
John Holloway		3/10/62	
William Patton		3/10/62	
Henry Liles		3/10/62	
William Ragon		12/15/61	

MILLSAPS COMPANY.

Name	Age	Enlisted	
Capt. Mitchell R. Millsaps		8/10/61	
Lieut. Ezra H. Duncan		3/29/62	
A. L. Barger	18		
Jonathan A. Beaty	28	10/11/61	
Wm. H. Beaty	20	4/11/63	
Jacob Cooper	30	10/11/61	
Council Cooper	27	10/11/61	
Jas. R. Davis	24	4/16/63	
Eli Eastridge	24	3/25/63	
Daniel Garrett	27	3/25/63	
Garrett Hall, Sr.	55	10/10/61	
Preston O. Holloway	27	5/12/63	
Henry Hoover	28	10/11/61	
Benjamin S. Jack		6/4/63	
Henry Langley	18	5/12/63	
Nathan J. Melton	20	3/7/62	
Sampson Mullinix	18	2/1/62	
J. C. Regan		6/16/63	Not mustered in
George Roberson	18	5/16/63	
John Scott	18	5/28/63	
Jas. Shannon		6/3/63	
Wm. R. Silvey	26	4/16/63	
Joseph Stonecipher	18	6/30/63	
Jas. Ellis	20	12/31/62	Killed at Rogersville
Powhatan Stringfield	19	5/3/63	
Wm. Wright	28	10/1/62	
Sam W. Goddard	19	3/20/63	
Thomas Winningham		6/10/63	

All of this company except four were mustered in June 5, 1863, in Kentucky. Joseph Stonecipher was mustered into the regular command June 30, 1863; P. Stringfield, on May 3, 1863; Thos. Winningham, June 10, 1863, and Wm. Wright on March 11, 1864. This company was attached to the Second Tennessee Mounted Infantry, according to information at hand, and surrendered with the regiment at Rogersville, Tennessee, November 6, 1863, and were placed in Confederate prisons. Honeycutt's company was mustered in at the same time, served in the same regiment, and shared the same fate, being captured at Rogersville by the Confederate General Jones.

What is known as "Battery B" was raised by Capt. R. C. Crawford at Lexington, Ky., and defeated a body of Confederates at Jamestown, Tenn., under S. P. Carter, according to U. S. A. Adjt. Gen.'s report, made in 1866.

CHAPTER XVII

CRUEL DEEDS.

THE old people of this section know what is meant by war. Its heavy hand rested in full force throughout the whole mountain country. There is scarcely a public road in this section that has not been marked by the blood of a soldier.

If there is such a thing as the fortunes of war it certainly meant nothing to this county. Fentress and adjoining counties furnished a field for marauding bands. It is probable that there is not another section of the Union where the hardships of war were greater, and where greater deeds of cruelty were perpetrated.

This territory furnished both officers and men to both the Union and the Confederate armies. Others remained at home and attempted to protect themselves. This section was on the border between the free and slave states. Fentress County had but few slaves and the bitterest feelings were engendered on the day that the election on secession was held. Fighting and bloodshed occurred on the election grounds, and as a matter of course, the feeling grew more bitter when the war came on. Civil government was suspended. Political rivals became opposing military leaders in the war, and the people arrayed themselves on one side or the other. In some cases father was against son, and brother against brother. Thus the people were divided. When a man belonging to one side was killed the other side was anxious to retaliate. For every deed of cruelty the perpetrators had their excuse at the time. After the smoke of battle has cleared away the cruel features only are remembered and told. Both sides have their stories. Here are some of them:

A little boy was permitted by his mother to go to a neighbors and spend the night. His father and several of his relatives were in the army. The next morning some men came by. One of them called him out and shot and killed him. His mother grieved as long as she lived for her boy, whom she said

FENTRESS COUNTY HIGH SCHOOL

HOOD SCHOOL
FENTRESS CO.

A PASSING RELIC

GOOTMEYER SCHOOL HOUSE
FENTRESS CO.

left home happy, "With a bright, clean face, and his hair nicely combed." Next morning she saw him stained with his life blood, cold in death.

A NEGRO MURDERED.

Some soldiers passed a blacksmith shop and ordered their horses shod. An ignorant negro did not please them by some of his conduct. One of the men coolly and deliberately shot him down like a dog. While the negro was in the death struggle his assailant picked up a sledge hammer and crushed his skull, at the same time cursing him.

PRISONERS KILLED.

In a little skirmish one man said to another, calling him by name, "I will surrender to you, I know you will not kill me," at the same time holding up his hands in token of submission. The other cruelly answered, "Just see if I don't," as he deliberately took aim and shot the helpless soldier dead.

In another instance a small band came upon two men in turning the bend in a road. The two men dropped their guns and threw up their hands imploringly. While in this position they were shot to death without a chance for defense. The parties who did this were afterwards tried for the offense, in the Federal Court, and acquitted. It appeared that they had been ordered to kill the men at sight, which explained their strange act.

Some regular soldiers surrendered and were put to death for no other known reason than that they were on the "other side."

SAVED BY SUPERSTITION.

A boy was stood up by the roadside as a target for cruel bullets. Three times the leader snapped his pistol at the back of the boy's tender head, when the leader turned to his men and said: "Boys, it is not right to kill this boy, my pistol never was known to snap before." He then turned his pistol from the boy, so the story goes, and it fired as usual. So the boy was released.

A VICTIM OF REVENGE.

A boy was standing at the fence in front of his home talking with some soldiers. One of them asked him who he was. He misunderstood the soldier and gave the name of a hated leader of the opposing side to that of the soldier, and before an explanation could be made the helpless boy was shot to death by the cruel, heartless wretch.

A FAMILY MURDERED.

Four men—a father and his two sons and a brother—the father having been discharged from the army, being over age, another in the bed suffering with the fever, others attending him, were attacked by a small armed force and all murdered. No resistance was offered. The wife and mother of the murdered ones returned home and found them scattered about, all dead.

For years and years after the war this poor palsied woman would talk of this tragedy and cry.

Many other stories of this kind are told in this section, but you will agree that these are sufficient to show how far the spirit of revenge led people astray during the fratricidal strife from 1861 to 1865.

These tragedies are remembered with sadness instead of bitterness toward the offenders. These sacrifices, for such they were, are regarded as a necessary result of conditions that existed which were beyond human control.

The border warfare in Kansas and Nebraska over slavery in the fifties, furnishes a parallel, probably on a larger scale, but there was enough here to sadden every heart, and has no doubt softened the hearts of many. Now this section is filled with as neighbor-loving people as can be found anywhere.

CALVIN LOGSTON.

In 1868 a family, consisting of the grandmother, her daughter, and three grandchildren, the oldest of whom was about eight years old, lived in Fentress County. On one day in November the two women and the second child were found in their house murdered. The oldest child had been struck in the head with an ax, but finally recovered. The youngest child, an infant, was found unhurt. Calvin Logston and two women were indicted for the murder. Logston was tried and convicted, and sentenced to death by hanging. The case was appealed to the Supreme Court and a new trial was granted. The case was then transferred to Overton County and Logston was again convicted, principally on the testimony of the eight-year-old boy. The case was again appealed, but was this time confirmed by the Supreme Court and the sentence carried out. He was buried in the Jamestown cemetery, in low ground. Water stands upon the grave in winter.

CHAPTER XVIII

FENTRESS COUNTY IN OTHER WARS.
THE INDIAN WARS.

JESSE COBB, and perhaps others, fought under Jackson at the Horseshoe Bend in Alabama in 1814. The horseshoe is formed by a bend in the Tallapoosa River. It was called Tohopeka by the Indians. Here the Indians, after a series of defeats, made their final stand, believing that this spot was protected by the Great Spirit, and hence could not be taken by the whites (having been so taught by their prophets), they fortified themselves in this natural stronghold.

Jackson cut a road through a dense forest, known as Hickory Ground, leading from the Coosa River to the Tallapoosa.

After reaching the Indian fortifications a desperate battle took place. Eight or nine hundred warriors were killed. Among them lay the Indian warrior and prophet, Monahoe, who had claimed to be proof against the white man's bullet. It is said that he carried a drum and incited the Indians by its rattle, and his incantations, to deeds of cruelty and to reckless butcheries. Jackson had forty-nine killed and one hundred and fifty-four wounded. Sam Houston received three severe wounds in this battle. The Indians fought desperately, refusing to surrender. Only about twenty of their number escaped. This battle ended the Creek War. Weatherford, the educated half-breed chief, soon afterwards surrendered to Jackson.

In 1836 Tennessee was called upon to furnish two thousand soldiers for the Florida War. Four thousand offered their services. The Middle Tennesseans were commanded by Gen Robert Armstrong. Wm. B. McDonald, whose widow, Mrs. Mary Ellen McDonald, lives at Jamestown, served through this war. George S. Kington and George Tinch also served in this war.

John Sevier, from whom some of our people have descended, has the honor of having done more than any other man in achieving the final peace with the Cherokees and the Chickamaugas in East Tennessee. His services are familiar history and it is unnecessary to recite them here. This is also true of James Robertson, who has relatives in this county.

John Palser Conatser, Andrew Beaty, Nathaniel Evans, —— Choate, —— Young and Thomas Buck, ancestors of a great number of people in our county, were among the first settlers at Watauga and doubtless participated in the Indian wars in that region.

CHAPTER XIX

THE REVOLUTIONARY WAR.

WE are so far removed from the Revolution that it is difficult to ascertain just how many of our immediate ancestors took part in this immortal struggle. However, we find among them Andrew Beaty, the great grandfather of Hon. C. Beaty; Benjamin Davis, from whom W. A. Beaty and others claim ancestry; John Palser Conatser, the grandfather of Uncle Hickory Conatser; David Gentry, the grandfather of John Gentry, and John Smith the great-great grandfather of the author of this history.

Family tradition relates that John Smith was blown up in a gunpowder explosion in the battle of Charleston and severely wounded. It is also related that Andrew Beaty was bitten by a rattlesnake at the battle of King's Mountain.

Andrew Beaty, Benjamin Davis and John Palser Conatser, fought at Kings Mountain, October 7, 1780. Here a part of Cornwallis' force, under Ferguson, was captured, and the plan of the British to take a state a time was thus frustrated. This battle is generally regarded as the beginning of the end of British rule in the Thirteen Colonies.

WAR OF 1812.

As will be seen by reference to the personal sketches, relatives and ancestors of our citizens did service in the War of 1812. William I. Beaty, Elias Bowden, Wm. Gentry, Thomas Cooper, David Collier, and perhaps others, were with Jackson at the battle of New Orleans, January 8, 1815.

Packenham, who was trained under Wellington, led his army against Jackson with almost incredible loss, when compared with that of Jackson, the British loss being over two thousand, while the Americans had only thirteen killed. The battle was won mainly by Tennessee and Kentucky riflemen, who had but little military training. The British were probably the best trained soldiers in the world, and it is said had never known defeat. These facts made the victory more wonderful, although it was an unnecessary battle, the treaty of peace having been signed more than two weeks before. A ship was then bringing the glad news of peace, but it came too late.

The fame of Jackson and his Tennesseans spread everywhere, and the hero of the battle became a national character.

CHAPTER XX

THE MEXICAN WAR.

FENTRESS COUNTY furnished its full share of volunteers in the war between the United States and Mexico. Among those who served in this war were Bates Bledsoe, —— Stephens, a son of David Stephens, John Quincy McGhee, John Cobb, Scott Bledsoe, Riar York, J. F. Adkins, Daniel Singleton, James York and James Edwards.

Bates Bledsoe and —— Stephens were killed during the war. McGhee died at San Antonio, Texas. G. B. McGhee, editor Golden Age, Livingston, Tenn., a nephew of J. Q. McGhee, has in his possession a gold watch that was purchased by J. Q. in the city of Mexico while he was a soldier during the occupancy of that city by the Americans.

A company was made up in Overton County by J. R. Copeland, in which some Fentress countains were enlisted, but this company was not accepted, as it was not needed. President Polk called for a limited number of soldiers. Tennessee's portion was 2,800. Nearly 30,000 offered their services, over ten times the number called for.

The soldiers from this section went from here to New Orleans, and from there by water to Vera Cruz, and then with Scott to Mexico, taking part in the many victories along the way. The most important engagements were Vera Cruz, March 23, 1847; Cerro Gordo, Contreras, Cherubusco, Chapultepec and Mexico City, which was occupied by the Americans, September 13, 1847.

SPANISH-AMERICAN WAR, 1898.

After the sinking of the battleship Maine, February, 1898, many young men from this county volunteered their services to the United States in the war which followed.

Among those who took part in this war the following names have been gathered: James L. Buck, Marion Wright, Wayne J.

Johnson, Charles Johnson, John Johnson, Wheeler Johnson, Joseph N. Johnson, D. M. Smith, Sim Linder, Flem Boles, Jno. K. Beaty, David Hardin Beaty, Cullen Robertson, Fayette York, Oliver Stephens, Monroe Stephens, William Stephens, Thomas Price and Capt. E. M. Shelley.

All did service in Cuba, except Capt. Shelley, who was captain of a Kentucky company, which was held on the southern border of the United States.

Marion Wright, James Buck and the five Johnson boys (all sons of Dr. P. E. Johnson, now of Rockwood), after serving in Cuba were sent to the Philippines and took part in many skirmishes with the Filipinos before Aguanaldo's surrender.

Wheeler and John Johnson and Marion Wright are still in the Philippines, all having entered business there.

Sim Linder died of pneumonia, 1914. John K. Beaty, who was corporal of his company, died a few years after his return home. Oliver and Monroe Stephens died soon after they returned.

The principal service rendered by this company was in assisting Cuba to regain its normal condition. Many of the people were starving and had to be fed by the United States. The usual disorder following a civil war, with its suffering, prevailed all over the island.

Company H, Capt. Cordell Hull's company, to which most of the Fentress County boys belonged, was stationed at Trinidad, on the southern coast of Cuba. The following, gathered from letters written for the author by Wheeler W. Johnson and D. M. Smith, while stationed there, 1899, will furnish some information in regard to the company and to the conditions in Cuba at the time:

Most of the volunteers from Fentress County were under Capt. Cordell Hull in Company H. A few, however, were under Capt. John W. Staples. Those under Hull were recruited at Jamestown.

Company H, of the fourth regiment of Tennessee volunteers, was commanded by Captain Hull. The regiment was under the command of Col. Leroy Brown. It was first stationed at Knoxville, Tenn., remaining there from June 18 to November 28,

1898, when the regiment, under orders from the war department, boarded the train for Savannah, Ga., enroute to Cuba. They reached Savannah and went aboard the transport Manitoba on December 1st. After a voyage of six days, covering fourteen hundred miles, they reached the southern coast of Cuba. The voyage was one of intense interest to most of the regiment. Few of them had ever seen the ocean. They were very much interested in the three Spanish men-of-war they saw on the coast of Cuba, having been wrecked by Senior Officer Schley, acting in the absence of Admiral Sampson, as the ships attempted to make their escape from the harbor in Santiago.

The regiment was landed at the old Spanish city of Trinidad, on the southern coast of Cuba, and assigned to garrison duty at that place.

The sanitary condition of the city was terrible. Dead and decaying animals and filth of every kind filled the streets. The buzzards flew unmolested about the streets and gathered food, sometimes coming into the mess kits of the soldiers for food. About two years before the United States declared war against Spain the Spaniards had issued a concentration order, by which the Cubans under arms were to come into the cities and give up their arms. These cities had been enclosed by high wire fences, and were further protected by block houses. No one was allowed to leave these enclosed places. Here they were held prisoners and furnished with very little food. Thus they were slowly but surely starved to death at our very door. Many died every day. It was common for the starving Cubans to eat from the swill pails of the American soldiers. Trinidad, under these conditions, in two years had decreased from about thirty to about ten thousand. The great work of the fourth regiment and of other United States soldiers at this time was to bring relief to these stricken people. Shortly after they reached Trinidad the United States issued rations for the Cubans, and the great work of humanity began. When the regiment left Cuba on March 25, 1899, the condition of the city and of the whole island had much improved and suffering soon ended.

The good ship Dixie brought the regiment to Savannah, where they were safely landed. On May 6, 1899, they were mustered out of service. Some of the regiment had given up their lives in Cuba, others came home with injured health to die. Among them was John K. Beaty, Corporal in Company H, and Oliver Stephens, Sim Linder and Monroe Stephens, all of whom served their country faithfully, and are worthy to be remembered as heroes of the Spanish-American War.

FENTRESS COUNTY IN THE PHILIPPINES.

On May 8, 1899, after serving with fourth regiment in Cuba, I enlisted in the regular army and was assigned to Company "M", Sixth U. S. Infantry, and on May 22, 1899, the regiment, commanded by Col. Charles Miner, went aboard the U. S. A. transport Sherman for service in the Philippine Islands, where we arrived on June 18, 1899. After several days of impatient waiting in Manila Bay we received orders to proceed to the islands of Panay, Negros, and Cebu. On July 4, 1899, we went ashore for the first time in one month and twelve days.

After landing we took an active part in suppressing the insurrection, which continued for about two years, until the capture of Aguanaldo, the insurrecto chief, which was accomplished on the island of Luzon, near what is now the "Summer Capital" of the Philippines, known as Boguio.

The insurrection was not, perhaps, what a great many people think it was. The fighting was not severe, yet we had many engagements of a small nature. But considering the fact that we were so far away from home, and in a strange land, and the hard marching through the mud and water—of which there was an abundance—and contending with the mosquitoes—of which there were also an abundance—poor food and bad water, and the hardships in general, service in the Philippines was no child's play.

After Aguanaldo was captured the backbone of the insurrection was broken, civil government was established throughout the archipelago in the latter part of 1902. Then the Moro people were to deal with, which required an expedition, in which I served. From the latter part of 1903 to the early part of 1905, there was ever-and-anon trouble and some fighting.

The trouble with the Moros was confined to the island of Mindanao and Jolo. As I served about fourteen years in the islands it was my good fortune to take a part in about all the fighting that took place in the islands against the insurrectos, which were the Filipinos, 1899 to 1902, and the Moros, 1899 to 1914.

In May, 1902, the first trouble of any consequence, I believe, took place at Lake Lanao, Mindanas, with some severe fighting, and has been going on more or less all the time since that date. Then, in what is known in the Cottabatto Valley, on the same island, the Moros gave the American authorities some trouble.

In 1904 an expedition was sent against hostile tribes of Moros and about 34% of the company to which I belonged were killed, and in the engagement I was slightly wounded.

In 1911-1913 some severe fighting took place on the Island of Jolo, at what is known as Bud Dajo and Bagsak, in which my brother, John L. Johnson, took a part, and in which several American soldiers lost their lives. At the time I left the Islands, a retired soldier (October 9, 1915), all was peace and tranquility, with a few minor exceptions.

Under American rule general prosperity exists and the Islands are blessed with good public schools and the people appear to be very well satisfied.

WHEELER W. JOHNSON,
A native of Fentress County.

CHAPTER XXI

THE INDIANS.

THE Indians lived in this section when the white people first came here. An Indian trace passed through the county and through Jamestown, and from Jamestown eastwardly along the divide between Yellow and White Oak creeks. There are places where it can be seen at this time. This was no doubt used by the Cherokees in going from East Tennessee to the Cumberland River regions, where the Shawnees once lived.

It is probable that Indian villages were at one time located on Yellow Creek, and possibly at Jamestown. On the farms of James Conatser and B. R. Stockton, there are evidences of the fact that Indians have spent much time in that region. Under bluffs on these farms there are immense piles of ashes, in which have been found many Indian relics, and more than a dozen skeletons, or the bones, rather, of more than a dozen Indians. The photograph in this book is from skulls and relics taken from under a bluff on the Conatser farm. The disfigured jaw of one, and the broken leg of another, show the hardships undergone by these Indians in their lifetime. The jaw appears to have been shot, the shot bursting off half the under jaw and passing through the mouth and cleaving off the upper jaw of the other side even with the palate, leaving no teeth in either jaw. It had healed perfectly, the jaw being perfectly smooth. The leg of the other had also knit together in good shape and was practically the same length of the other.

The bones that are found are usually well preserved, having been buried under a dry cliff and covered with ashes.

Samuel Walker, of Scott County, one of the soldiers who assisted in the removal of the Indians west of the Mississippi, in talking with the author, said that the Indians had learned the English language, and many of them were living like the white people, and courted and intermarried with the whites; but that there was a great irreconcilable difference between the two races that made it impossible for both to live together. The Indian would not consent to abandon his tribal government. He insisted that the Indian should be tried for his offenses by the Indian council, and that the white man should be tried by the white man, and rather than consent to any other arrangement he parted with his old home forever.

The Indians were finally removed in 1842. Mr. Walker was about eighteen years old. He told an amusing story connected with his service in this work of removal. One day he was on picket duty with orders to allow no one to pass either in or out of the lines. A white man and an Indian maiden were seated on a log within the lines talking. They would talk awhile and cry awhile. This attracted the attention of Mr. Walker so much that he forgot his duty as a picket, and while he was engaged watching the couple on the log an Indian slipped through the lines and was forty yards away before Mr. Walker discovered him. He raised his gun and called on the Indian to halt, but the Indian only ran the faster. He took his gun from his shoulder and let the Indian go, feeling that it was his fault that he had allowed the Indian to get through the lines. In a few minutes the Indian returned with a little bundle and again passed through the lines. Soon they were all on their way.

The Indians were first collected at Knoxville. An old Indian, who was being taken to Knoxville preparatory to removal, objected to the course being taken and said: "This is not the way to Arkansas." The officer answered: "Move on, I'll get you to Arkansas all right."

CHAPTER XXII

JIM CROCKETT.

IT is related that a little deaf and dumb boy, named Jim Crockett, was taken captive by the Indians and kept by them for a number of years. He and his brother Joe were cutting wood near where Harve Smith now lives. The Indians came upon them. Joe heard them and ran. They shot him and broke his arm, but he managed to get away. The deaf and dumb boy was captured by them and held by them until finally exchanged for an Indian the whites had captured. While this boy was a prisoner it is said that he would be taken by the Indians to a point near a lead mine on the East Fork, where they would tie him and leave him until they would go and get a load for him and themselves. He was never allowed to see the mine, and it has never been found.

Joe's arm was taken off below the elbow, and it is a part of the story that an iron cuff was put upon the end of his arm. In this he would put the handle of a fork and use it at the table while eating.

The story which is here related of Joe Crockett as happening in Fentress County is believed to be true, for the reason that William Crockett, an uncle of Davy Crockett, lived in the pioneer days at what is now known as the Jerry Beaty farm, near where Joe was captured. The Beaty's, who are related to Crockett, also moved into this very neighborhood. The story is told with much detail by those who have heard the story from their ancestors, who claimed to have seen both Joe and James. However, Davy Crockett's history contains the same story, but fixes the location in Hawkins County, and locates his uncle William in Kentucky, in which he is doubtless mistaken. The boundary line of Kentucky and Tennessee was, long after Davy's death, a matter of dispute, and the county boundary lines were not well defined, hence the possibility of a mistake.

THE RED DEER.

It is related that a man was once passing through this country with a sack of gold. His horse broke his leg above a cliff. The load being too great for the man to carry he went below the cliff and hid his sack of gold. On the cliff he carved a red deer, so that he might return and find the money. It is said that he went on his way and never returned. It is also said that many a futile search has been made for the cliff with the "Red Deer." The story has at least served to interest children and possibly has aroused the spirit in some that led the ancients to chase the rainbow with the hope of finding a pot of gold.

HORSE RACING.

Before the war race tracks were common. There was one in what is now the northern part of Jamestown, which was the scene of many exciting races. Betting was common; in fact, the life of the races and the race track. Edward Franklin, Edward Paul and Staples, of Morgan County, seem to have been the leaders.

One of these men owned a filly that sold for seven hundred dollars. She became famous on the rack track. She was taken to Georgia and finally to California.

CUMBERLAND MOUNTAIN LOOM

INDIAN RELICS, JAMES CONATSER FARM
NEAR JAMESTOWN

BAPTIZING IN THE BEAUTIFUL CLEAR FORK RIVER

CHAPTER XXIII

MARSHA MILLSAP'S CASE.

State of Tennessee
    vs. } Libel
William M. Bledsoe.

Page 356, Minute Book, Circuit Court Record, Fentress County, June term of the Circuit Court, 1843.

To whom it may concern:

CAUTION.

A witch of the most extraordinary power has made her appearance in Jamestown. She can, at a single touch, convert those who have lived without stain or blemish into the most consummate rogues and rascals. She can transform members of the church into liars, sorcerers and robbers of hen roosts. She can change her neighbors' geese into her own with a single touch of her all-powerful wand. She infects those who share her bed with an overstock of loathsome vermin. She fills those with whom she converses with false ideas of her neighbor's honesty. She can transform herself into a suitable mate for the masculine gender of the canine species, which she has fully tested by experiment.

Unless she ceases the exercise of the diabolical art she shall feel the force of public opinion turned against her.

(Signed) A. WIZZARD.

A true bill was found against Bledsoe for libeling Marsha Millsaps, John H. Savage being the attorney general. He was found guilty and fined $25 and costs.

A short time afterwards Marsha Millsaps and her husband, Hiram Millsaps, filed two damage suits against William M. Bledsoe and Robert H. MacIlvain, respectively, for $10,000 each for circulating above defamatory and libelous matter. The jury, Thomas Choate, John Culver, Fuller Grisham, Joseph Upchurch, Francis Davidson, James Story, William C. Davidson, David Crawford, Archibald Dishman, Abraham Terry, Martin Crouch and Joseph Wilson rendered judgment in favor of Marsha in the sum of $10,000 damages in each case.

MacIlvain then brought suit against Hiram Millsaps and his wife Marsha for $5,000 damages for falsely charging him with mutilating the books in the Register's office, of which he had charge. The jury gave judgment in his favor for the full amount claimed. In all these cases the judgment seems to have been released by the winners upon the payment of the costs.

JOHNS VS. MACE.

From the records in the Circuit Court in a case styled Eli F. Johns vs. Phillips Mace, some items in the accounts filed in the case are interesting.

1841—Phillip Mace, credit by boat, $40.
      By two kegs of tar, $2.
      By two gallons of liquor, at 50c, $1.
      To one quart of whiskey and six pounds of pork, 80c.
      To one deer skin on the river, 75c.
      To two ounces of indigo, 40c.
      To one gallon of whiskey, by Mathew Pennicuff, 50c.
      To five and one-half pints of whiskey, $31\frac{1}{4}$c.

STATE VS. JULIAN F. SCOTT.

Julian F. Scott was indicted for not keeping Scott's Turnpike, the road leading from Jamestown toward Clarkrange, which he owned, in proper repair, and found guilty and fined $5 at the June term of the Circuit Court in 1844.

The case was tried by Joel Hinds, William Lee, John Price, Andrew Conatser, Kaleb Stephens, Robert Boles, Elisha Hood, Arthur Edwards, John Linder, Mathew Wood, John Albertson and Perry Pulse as jurymen.

This road was much traveled in the days of slavery. Stock was carried south over this road and exchanged for slaves.

CHAPTER XXIV

THE ONLY WITCHCRAFT CASE IN TENNESSEE.

FIFTEEN or twenty years ago the following appeared as a news item, under the above head, in the Chattanooga Times:

"The official records have been received in this city, as a matter of historical interest, of the first and only arrest and prosecution for witchcraft ever had in Tennessee. The scene was Jamestown, Fentress County, claimed by many to be the Obedstown of Mark Twain, and by many of the older residents to be the actual birthplace of Mark Twain, whose father was at one time Circuit Court Clerk of Fentress County, and a practicing lawyer at the bar.

"The case of witchcraft was in the year 1835, and originated on the banks of the Obeys River, the trial being before Joshua Owens, a Justice of the Peace.

"An old man named Stout, who lived in a very quiet way in the neighborhood, who did not attend church, who had been sitting up late at nights reading strange books, and about whose early history nothing was known, was suspected of being a witch, and when a daughter of one Taylor was taken violently ill with a disease that the doctor could not diagnose, it was determined to arrest old man Stout for bewitching her.

"A large posse was secured, and guns were loaded with silver bullets, as it was thought that nothing else would kill a witch.

"The old man was arrested and brought to trial before Squire Owens. A vast array of witnesses testified as to his habits, and added that they had seen him escape from dwelling houses through the keyhole in the doors, and that he had thrown people and animals into strange spells by his influence when they were miles away from him. The officers and posse subjected him to a great many indignities, and he was held to await the action of the grand jury.

"When court convened Judge Abraham Caruthers, who was on the bench, and Gen. Jno. B. McCormick, the prosecuting attorney, refused to indict the old man, the action of the court and attorney general almost precipitated a riot in the court room.

"Old man Stout then sued the officers and posse for damages, and they pleaded as a defense that they were in the act of arraigning a criminal, and cited the statute of Henry VIII and James I, making witchcraft a felony, which they declared had never been repealed in Tennessee. Judge Caruthers, however, charged the jury that these statutes were repugnant to and destructive of the freedom of the State, and to a republican form of government, and by the act of 1778 never in effect in Tennessee. Thus ended the first trial of a person charged with witchcraft in Tennessee by the conviction of the persons who had arrested him and subjected him to great indignities."

The above article was clipped from the Times and preserved by the author of this book. The statements with reference to the facts in the case and the charge and action of the court are undoubtedly in the main true, but can not be verified by the records in the Circuit Clerk's office. The records covering this period are missing. They were probably burned in the fire which consumed the courthouse and part of the contents in 1905.

Under the statute of Henry VIII, referred to in this article, all witchcraft and sorcery was a felony without benefit of clergy, and Blackstone, in his Commentaries under the head, "Crimes Against God and Religion," says: "Witchcraft is a sixth species of offense, and to deny it is to deny the revealed word of God."

Scarcely two centuries ago the main body of Christians believed in witchcraft, and under the solemn sanction of the law, hundreds of poor old decrepit women, condemned as witches, were tortured and died amidst the blazing fagots. It has been said that the lurid light of these judicial fires is spread upon the pages of American history. Some of the greatest and wisest men believed in this delusion. Francis

Bacon, Sir Mathew Hale, Martin Luther, John Wesley and Cotton Mather were among the many professed believers. Great theologians contended that disbelief in witchcraft was rank heresy and cited the scriptures: "Thou shalt not suffer a witch to live."—Exodus 22:18.

Louis XIV, during his reign, stopped prosecutions in France for witchery. This was followed by an English statute, enacted under George II. This statute declared "That no prosecution shall, for the future, be carried on against any person for conjuration, witchcraft, sorcery or enchantment."

It is proper to say that Fentress County is as free from ideas of witchcraft and superstition as any of her sister counties. People everywhere inherit more or less superstition, and a person perfectly free from superstition would probably be hard to find. This is not strange when we consider how short the time has been since our ancestors gave the solemn sanction of the law to superstitious ideas.

The following case, taken from Vol. VII of Chadman's Encyclopedia of Law, illustrates the peculiarities of some people along this line:

MATTER OF VEDDER.

This case was brought to break a will. It was proved that the testatrix was very old, and in a gradually failing condition; that she put irons in the cream, and marked the bottom of the churn with the sign of the cross to make the butter come; that she said she could not keep her horses fat because the witches rode them at night; that she told a neighbor that she had seen a headless horseman riding across the field; that she told another neighbor that her crying child was bewitched; that if she would search its pillow she would find a hard bunch of feathers, which was the witch; that she should boil this bunch at night in a pot, and that at midnight she would hear some one knock, that she should not answer, and in the morning the body of the witch would be found outside the door; that she told a certain woman to put live coals and a red garter under her churn to make the butter come; that once upon a time she took her nephew (a contestant) to dig for gold upon her farm, and had him carry a red rooster under his arm for good luck, and that they dug and found no gold; that she said that she desired to be robed like the angels when she died. All these things happened in the last quarter of a century of her life. She proved that she used good judgment in her business affairs and the will was upheld.

SUGGESTIVE QUESTIONS FOR TEACHERS

CHAPTER I.

Locate Fentress County. In what natural division does it principally lie? Bound it. Give its area and population. When and where was it created? How? For whom was it named? What is the county seat? What was it once called? What is it called in the Gilded Age? How was the place connected with Indian history? When was the first courthouse built? When was it first incorporated? What is the population of the town? To what race do they belong? Tell what you can of the population of the county.

CHAPTER II.

Describe the surface of the county. Give the three principal natural divisions. Describe the soil of each division. Mention some products that have been successfully grown. Mention some crops and give amount produced on the acre. Mention some of the natural advantages of the plateau. What can you say of cattle raising on the plateau? What was the first industry of the people who lived on the plateau?

Name some of the pioneers in the Wolf River region. Where were the first courts held in the county? For whom was the Obeys River named? Who were the Long Hunters? Describe Rock Castle. What minerals are found? Mention some of the natural curiosities of the Castle.

CHAPTER III.

Why does the writer call Jamestown a quaint old town? Mention some of the changes that have taken place. What mistakes are made by the writer in this article? Who was Wade Erwin? What important public buildings have been erected within the past few years?

CHAPTER IV.

Who drew the first plan for a courthouse and jail for this county? Describe the jail to be built. Describe the plan for the courthouse. What was the date fixed for the completion of these buildings.

CHAPTER V.

Who was Mark Twain? In what way is his history connected with Fentress County? What official position did his father hold in the county? Who wrote the Gilded Age? Why is it of special interest to us? In what sense is it true? Who was Si Hawkins? How did the Clemons heirs obtain title to so much land in Fentress County? What interests you most in this chapter?

CHAPTER VI.

Name some of the officers who served in the Fourth Tennessee Cavalry. Give some officers who were natives of the county. What Fentress countian was finally a commander of the regiment? Under what famous cavalry leader did they serve? Mention some other Tennessee counties that were associated with Fentress in the war.

CHAPTER VII.

Where was Bledsoe's company formed? Where was their first service? To what great general were they ordered to report early in the war? Mention some battles in which they took part.

CHAPTER VIII.

Where was their first engagement after their transfer to the Fourth Tennessee Cavalry? Describe the battle of Murfreesboro. Mention some Fentress County soldiers who were killed at McMinnville. At Fort Donelson. Describe the battle of Chickamauga.

CHAPTER IX.

Give the date of Wheeler's raid, and the results. Who were among the killed?

CHAPTER X.

Who were the first to resist Sherman in his famous march? Mention and describe some of the battles in Georgia in which the Fourth Tennessee took part.

CHAPTER XI.

Describe the battle of Saltville. Tell of Gen. Williams. Who was Champ Ferguson? Tell of Lieut. Smith.

CHAPTER XII.

Describe Sherman's march from Atlanta to the sea. From Savannah through the Carolinas. What is said of the killed and wounded in this campaign?

CHAPTER XIII.

Describe the surrender of the Fourth Tennessee. Why were there so few to be mustered out at Greensboro and Charlotte? Repeat some sentences from Wheeler's Farewell Address that are of interest.

CHAPTER XIV.

Tell of the Bledsoes. Tell of others who distinguished themselves in the war.

CHAPTER XV.

Name three Union commanders who were natives of Fentress County. Tell something of each of them.

CHAPTER XVI.

Where was the Second East Tennessee Regiment recruited? Mention some of the officers of this regiment. Describe some of the most important engagements in which they took part. Where were they captured by the Confederates? Where were they imprisoned? Were any of your relatives in this command? Mention some who gave up their life in this service.

CHAPTER XVII.

Why did Fentress County suffer so heavily the effects of the war?

CHAPTER XVIII.

Why is the battle of the Horseshoe Bend of peculiar interest to us? Describe this battle. What two great Tennesseans took part in this battle? Mention some Fentress countains that took part in this battle. Tell of the Florida war. What connection did the people of our county have with it? What connection between some of our early ancestors and John Sevier?

CHAPTER XIX.

Mention some of our ancestry that took part in the Revolution. Battle of Kings Mountain. Describe this battle. Give names of some soldiers of the War of 1812. Under whom did they serve? In what great battle did they take part? Describe the battle.

CHAPTER XX.

Name ten Fentress countains who served in the Mexican War. What can you say of J. Q. McGhee? Mention the important engagements. Describe them. When was Mexico City occupied? What caused the war with Spain in 1898? Mention some volunteers from this county. Mention some who were sent to the Philippines. What was their principal work in Cuba? Who was their captain? Tell something of the condition of Cuba at the time.

CHAPTER XXI.

Tell what you can of the Indians that lived here. What evidences have we of their former life here? Tell Mr. Walker's story of their removal beyond the Mississippi. Tell the Story of Jim Crockett. Tell the story of the Red Deer.

CHAPTER XXIII.

What interesting lawsuits are described in this chapter? What is peculiar in Eli F. John's account against Mace? Where is Scott's Turnpike? Why so called?

CHAPTER XXIV.

What was the only witchcraft case that was ever tried in Tennessee? Who were the parties? What Justice of the Peace tried the case? What famous judge finally disposed of it? Who was the attorney general? When were the witchcraft laws repealed? Tell the important feature of the Vedder case.

PART TWO

PART TWO

PERSONAL SKETCHES

ELIAS BOWDEN.

ELIAS BOWDEN was the son of John Bowden, a native of Franklin County, North Carolina. When a young man he enlisted in the army and served five years, which included the war of 1812 with England. After the war he was sent with the command to drive the whites off the Indian lands in East Tennessee, or Georgia; later was sent to Missouri, and was at St. Louis, then a fort, having been one of the old French forts. They went from there up the Missouri to make a treaty with the Indians. At the end of the five years he was discharged, and in 1818 came to Fentress County and hired to work to Bailey Owen, who lived near Boatland on the East Fork of Obeds River. Soon afterwards he married Mary Owen, a daughter of Bailey Owen. He bought and settled the farm where Perry Hinds now lives below Boatland. He and his wife spent the remainder of their lives on this farm, and were buried at what is now the Dr. Chism cemetery.

Eight children were born to them—three girls and five boys —viz., Polly, Miley and Nicey Ann; William B., Joshua S., Elias W., Bailey O. and Sampson V.

Polly Bowden married Clark Franklin, a tailor. She died in Kentucky.

Miley married Gwyn Stephens, a farmer. They lived for awhile on Cumberland Mountain, in the south end of the county, and later moved to Kentucky, where they both died many years ago.

Nicey Ann married Granville Gwyn. They went to Missouri, then to Texas, and died there.

W. B. BOWDEN.

W. B. Bowden was trustee of Fentress County two terms, and served one term as a member of the State Legislature in the latter part of the 70's. He was a member of the county court for many years.

He married Sallie Franklin, and lived on a farm he owned on the river above Boatland, now owned by James E. Beaty. He and his wife are both buried in the cemetery on this farm. Near the cemetery is an Indian mound, from which some Indian relics have been taken.

Mr. Bowden was a very clever man and much loved by his neighbors. It is said that he never laughed nor cried. He sometimes smiled, but never laughed aloud, yet he was always pleasant and agreeable. He read a great deal and kept well informed.

JOSHUA BOWDEN.

Joshua Bowden married Polly Ann Stephens, who is still living. He was a farmer and a shoe and boot maker. He taught school for several years when a young man. He died on his farm near Glenobey a few years ago.

ELIAS W. BOWDEN.

E. W. Bowden married Emma Mullinix, a daughter of Eli Mullinix. He followed farming, and lived on the old Elias Bowden farm until shortly before his death a few years ago. He served for several years as Justice of the Peace in the first district. His widow is still living.

SAMPSON V. BOWDEN.

S. V. Bowden lived on the farm until he went with his brother, B. O. Bowden, to Mt. Cumberland and Hiawassee College.

He was elected a member of the legislature in 1861, and after the fall of Fort Donaldson, in 1862, he went with the legislature to Memphis, at the request of the Governor, Isham G. Harris. He succeeded his brother, B. O. Bowden, as Clerk and Master of Fentress County. He studied and practiced law at Jamestown. Later he became a clerk in the pension office at Knoxville, and served fourteen years. He died in Knoxville a few years ago and was buried in Gay cemetery.

BAILEY OWEN BOWDEN.

B. O. Bowden was born in 1834, near Boatland. He worked on the farm with his father, Elias Bowden, until he was twenty-two. He then entered Mount Cumberland Academy, which was located in the Poplar Cove in Fentress County, and attended three sessions. He then went to Hiawassee College, walking eighty-five miles to reach the school. He remained in this school two years and six months, when the Civil War broke out. He then enlisted in the Federal army and served to the close of the war, and took part in the battles of Nashville, Franklin and others.

He was the first Clerk and Master in Fentress County after the war, receiving his appointment in 1865. In 1867 he was married to Mary Catherine Sproul, a graduate of Rogersville Female College. After serving as Clerk and Master, he went to Hiawassee College and taught seven years in that institution. He taught two years at Columbus, Kansas, and six years, from 1888 to 1894, at Alpine Institute, in Overton County, Tennessee. His wife and his daughter, Nora Deane Roberts, and his son-in-law, Hon. A. H. Roberts, the present Chancellor Judge of this district, were associated with him in this school. This school, under their management, became the most valuable educational institution in the mountain country. Many men and women in Fentress and adjoining counties owe their success to this institution.

B. O. Bowden lives at Livingston, Tennessee.

JOSHUA OWEN.

Joshua Owen was the son of Bailey Owen, who was a pioneer settler on the East Fork, below Boatland, where Joshua was born, and spent his long and useful life. He married a daughter of John Beaty, another pioneer. He was a Justice of the Peace for many years. It is doubtful if anyone ever held the office longer, or performed a greater number of marriage ceremonies, than he did. He also tried the celebrated witchcraft case, an account of which has already been given.

He and his wife lie buried in the old Bowden cemetery, near Dr. Chism's.

DR. JOHN NEWTON CHISM.

Dr. Chism was born in Kentucky in 1853, and came to Tennessee in 1884. His father was William G. Chism, and his mother was Elizabeth (Ray) Chism. His ancestors came from England.

He took the medical course at Vanderbilt, and has practiced successfully for over a quarter of a century.

He is a member of the Baptist Church, and is a Mason and an Odd Fellow. He is a democrat.

He was married to Martha J. Wood, a daughter of Jerry Wood, in 1906.

He owns and operates, with success, a large farm near Boatland, where he resides.

LAWRENCE BREED CHISM.

L. B. Chism was born in Monroe County, Kentucky, 1850, and attended school at Tompkinsville with Ex-Governor Benton McMillin. Later he was a student at Valparaiso, Indiana. He taught school six years in Kentucky, and came to Tennessee in 1884 and engaged in the mercantile business, and has followed this successfully ever since. He now resides at Little Crab.

He was elected and served eight years as County Judge of Fentress County. He was postmaster at Little Crab during Cleveland's administration and deputy during Roosevelt's.

He became a member of the Baptist Church in 1893, and was ordained a minister in 1905.

He married Mary Wood in 1888, a daughter of Jerry Wood, who was for a long time a merchant and Postmaster at Boatland. He is a brother of Dr. J. N. Chism, and received his name from his great grandmother Breed, and his great-grandfather Lawrence Gillock. He is a Mason and a democrat.

BAILEY W. BOWDEN, JR.

Bailey W. Bowden, Jr., is a son of Joshua Bowden, and was born in 1868, near Glenoby, on the East Fork, where he now lives. Zoral Stephens and Susie Stephens were his grandparents on his mother's side. They came from North Carolina, and became a part of the first settlers of the Buffalo Cove. Stephens entered a large amount of land.

B. W. was educated at Alpine and taught for several years; is now postmaster at Glenoby, and is a farmer and blacksmith. He has served a term as a Justice of the Peace, and one as a member of the County Board of Education. He is a member of the M. E. Church, a Mason and an Odd Fellow. Democrat.

He married Leva Ann Tompkins in 1893, a daughter of J. M. Tompkins, who was for a long time postmaster at Armathwaite, and a leading citizen of the tenth district.

DILLARD OSBORNE BEATY.

D. O. Beaty was born near Little Crab in 1890, and is a son of Lewis Beaty and a grandson of John Beaty and Elias W. Bowden, q. v.

Has attended Pleasant Hill Academy, Fentress County High School and Athens Business College, Athens, Ga. Taught school successfully several years in Fentress and in Pickett counties. Is now Deputy Clerk and Master, Fentress County, and works as a stenographer.

He is a Royal Arch Mason and an Odd Fellow, member of M. E. Church, South, holds license to practice law in the justice's and in the county court of the county.

RUFUS J. STEPHENS. 1848.

R. J. Stephens is the son of Gwyn Stephens and Miley Bowden. His grandfather and grandmother were David and Sarah Stephens. His great-grandfather, Thomas Stephens, came from South Carolina to Fentress County and became one of the pioneer settlers.

On his mother's side his grandfather was Elias Bowden, q. v. John Bowden, his great-grandfather, came from England and settled in Franklin County, North Carolina.

He was married to Sarah E. Mullinix in 1872. She was a daughter of Eli Mullinix. He has two sons—Sylvester and Jasper—both of whom have taught school in this county.

He is a member of the Masonic Lodge, at Clarkrange, and he and his wife are members of the M. E. Church.

He owns and operates a nice farm on the river below Boatland. He has a large number of colonies of bees and sells honey nearly every year.

ISAIAH STEPHENS. 1837.

Isaiah Stephens lives on the breaks of the Cumberland Plateau, ten miles south of Jamestown, and is a native of the county. His father was David Stephens. Grandfather Thomas Stephens came to Fentress County from near the South Carolina coast when this section was a wilderness. His mother, Sarah Long, was born in South Carolina, and came with her father, Henry Long, and settled on Indian Creek on a part of what is now the J. C. Smith Farm. Indians were then plentiful on this creek. From this fact the creek derived its name.

He is a member of the M. E. Church. He was married to Polly Ann Greer in 1863 and Sarah Hood in 1898.

One of his brothers was a soldier in the Mexican War and died in the service. John, Russell, David and Edward Stephens were his other brothers, and are the ancestors of nearly all the Stephen's now living in the county. All have been farmers, and respected, law-abiding citizens of the county.

JAMES ALVIN HOOD. 1872.

Alvin Hood lives on the East Fork in the southern part of the county, where he was born. He is a son of Solomon Hood, a grandson of Elisha Hood, great-grandson of Andy Hood, who came from North Carolina with his family and was the first settler on Bill's Creek, settling at the mouth of the creek. Some very old apple trees are still standing to mark the spot.

Andy died about 1850. His son, Elisha, was born 1803 and died in 1889 on the East Fork and was buried there. He had five sons—Jeremiah, Thomas, Solomon, Zephaniah and John, all of whom are dead. The Hood family, who live in the southern part of the county, are the descendants of these five brothers.

Alvin and his brothers—Seymour and Anderson—have taught school. They attended the Jamestown school.

Alvin is a member of the M. E. Church, South, and a democrat.

JESSE W. EVANS.

J. W. Evans was born near Rugby, Tennessee, in 1861, and is the son of Samuel and Deborah Evans, and a grandson of Nathan Evans and Jesse Cobb. His grandfather Cobb was a cousin of Howell E. Cobb, of Georgia, who served as speaker of the National House of Representatives in 1850, was Secretary of the Treasury under Buchanan, and Governor of Georgia.

Evans was raised on a farm; began life as a teacher; was Deputy Sheriff two years; Circuit Court Clerk four years, and has been County Attorney since 1910, having been appointed by Governor Hooper in 1910 and elected over two competitors in 1912. He is a successful lawyer, and was admitted to the bar in 1890. He was married the same year to Miss Dean Delk. He is an Odd Fellow. Republican in politics.

His father, Samuel Evans, was a soldier in the Union army during the Civil War, serving in the Second Tennessee Regiment. Was captured at Rogersville and imprisoned thirteen months on Bell's Island. He died at Murfreesboro in 1865.

His grandfather, Nathan Evans, came to this county from North Carolina soon after Tennessee was admitted to the Union and opened up a farm on Caney Creek, on Wolf River, and here raised a large family. He was a cousin of the Nathan Evans who assisted John Sevier in escaping from the North Carolina authorities. He married a sister of Joshua and Jas. Story. Joshua settled on Crab, at what is now known as the George Beaty place. James settled on Caney Creek, near Evans.

Jesse Cobb came from Tuscaloosa, Ala., in about 1818. He married a Stephens and settled in the Poplar Cove, where the Cobb's have since resided. He was Register of the county before the war and a well-to-do farmer.

He fought under Jackson at the battle of the Horseshoe Bend. He was a democrat and attended the convention that instructed the State for James K. Polk. He was associated with Attorney General John B. McCormack in building a mill on the East Fork near where J. P. Culver lives. Five thousand dollars was borrowed by them from a Sparta bank to carry on the work. A huge dam was built across the river at great expense, the remains of which can yet be seen, but it soon washed away and the mill project was abandoned. When the notes fell due Cobb was compelled to pay them, which he did by taking a drove of mules to Georgia each year for five years, paying a thousand dollars each year, in accordance with a compromise in Circuit Court of Fentress County.

He died in 1864 on Wolf River and was buried in the old Evans cemetery.

MATHIAS WRIGHT. 1818-1899.

M. Wright came from Greene County and settled near Little Crab. He was for many years a deacon in the Cedar Grove Baptist Church at Little Crab, and was postmaster there for a long time. He sawed and delivered some of the lumber that was used in the Capitol building at Nashville.

For several years he was County Trustee of Fentress County. While serving as Trustee he was assaulted by some robbers and about four hundred dollars taken from him. The robbers tried to force him to tell where the rest of the county money was, but he refused to tell them and suffered them to hang him with a rope until he was almost lifeless. The robbers finally left him. Three of them were captured but later fled the country. Uncle Mathias' honesty saved the county over a thousand dollars, and he died with the confidence and respect of all who knew him.

JOHN W. GAUDIN.

John W. Gaudin was born in Lausanne, Switzerland; was educated in Paris, and became proficient in Latin, Greek, German and Italian, although French was his native tongue. He became a perfect English scholar after coming to the United States.

He came over to New York City at the age of eighteen, penniless. He worked as errand boy for a physician in that city for two years, then came to Knox County, Tennessee, and worked on a farm for two or three years, then to Morgan County and continued to work on the farm, finally marrying a girl who was also a native of Switzerland. They, together, went into the mercantile business on the old Montgomery road, eight miles east of the Gatewood ford of the Clear Fork River. They remained here until 1858, then sold out and came to Fentress County and went into merchandising three miles northwest of Jamestown, on the Wolf River Road. In 1861 he enlisted in the Federal Army and served to the close of the war in 1865; was Quartermaster General of his regiment. After the war he tried farming in the State of Illinois; his family having no health they came back to Fentress County in 1868 and again took up merchandising, this time in Jamestown; was appointed postmaster and continued at Jamestown until 1879, when he sold out and sailed back to Switzerland to visit friends and relatives and his native land. While there he visited the Alps and their greatest glaciers and many historic places of the Old World, returning again to Jamestown in 1881 and living a quiet and retired life until 1889, when he again emigrated, this time to the great San Joaquin Valley in California. Here he bought a small fruit farm and after one year sold it and moved into Amador County and bought a farm of three hundred and sixty acres, but in a year or so he lost his health; so he sold out and bought a home in the little town of Wallace on the S. & N. E. Railway in Amador County, and there died in 1892 and was buried by the G. A. R. at the cemetery near the city of Stockton.

WILLIAM J. GAUDIN. 1859.

W. J. Gaudin is the son of John W. and Adelia (Very) Gaudin. Was born in Fentress County in 1859. His grandparents were born, lived and died in Petit Chautane, Lausanne, Switzerland.

He received his education at Hiawassee College, and taught school, and held the office of County Superintendent of Schools for Fentress County; was appointed United States Commissioner in 1882, and has held the office ever since; was elected a member of the County Board of Education by an almost unanimous vote of the people of his district in 1912, but has since resigned. He has been in the mercantile business since 1892, and is also a successful up-to-date farmer, and has demonstrated the great possibilities of farming and truck raising on the plateau.

He is a 32° Mason and an I. O. O. F. Is a republican in politics and a member of the Methodist Church.

He was married to Zibbie A. Edwards in 1881, and to his present wife—Jennie A. Rich—in 1905, who is a daughter of Landon Rich, a member of the county court of the county for many years.

CYRIL CORNELIUS FROGGE. 1858.

C. C. Frogge was born on Wolf River in 1858, and is the son of John W. and Nancy (Wright) Frogge, and grandson of Cornelius M. and Deborah (Carpenter) Frogge, and John Wright and Penina (Dale) Wright, and a great-grandson of John Frogge, who was a first cousin of President James Madison of Virginia.

He received his educational training from the public schools and from Jamestown Academy, and has taught successfully for thirty-six consecutive years in the public schools of the county, all of which has been in his home district — the old seventh—with the exception of one year.

He is a democrat, and served his district as a Justice of the Peace from 1888 to 1894.

He became a member of the Methodist Church in early life, and was ordained a minister in 1893. He is well known all over the county in church and educational circles.

OCIE OSWELL FROGGE. 1894.

O. O. Frogge is the son of C. C. Frogge, q. v., and Mary E. (Riley) Frogge, a daughter of John Floyd Riley. He has received his education from the public schools and from the county high school. He began teaching at seventeen, and has taught at Reed's Creek, Frogge's Chapel, and is now teaching at Red Hill. He is one of the youngest teachers in the county, and has been very successful. He is a member of the Methodist Church.

WILLIAM DALEY HULL. 1878.

W. D. Hull was born near Shirley, where he now lives. He is the son of Lewis and Marilda Hull, a grandson of A. B. and Sirena Hull, and is a cousin of Congressman Hull.

Attended public schools and A. B. Wright Institute; began teaching in 1898, and is now teaching his eighth year. Was a member of the first County High School Board in the county, and served one term as a Justice of the Peace, 1906 to 1912.

He was married to Josie Buck, a daughter of Landon and Margaret J. Buck, in 1908.

JAMES T. BUCK. 1877.

J. T. Buck is a son of Noah and Amanda (Evans) Buck, grandson of Jonathan Buck, and a great-grandson of Thomas Buck, who emigrated to this county from Watauga in pioneer days. The Buck family came originally from England to Pennsylvania.

Attended the Rugby high school and has taught school eight years in the tenth and twelfth districts.

He was a soldier in the Spanish-American War serving in Co. K in Cuba, then went with Co. E to the Philippines, during the war there. He was in several skirmishes with the Filipinos and learned many interesting things about them and their country.

He was married to Belle Brooks, in 1902, after his return from the Philippines. He now lives near Armathwaite, and is teaching.

STANLEY HULL. 1892.

Parents: A. Y. and Mary A. (Brooks) Hull.

Paternal grandparents: A. B. and Sirna Hull.

Maternal grandparents: W. S. and Hulda (Allen) Brooks. Lives near Shirley.

Attended A. B. Wright Institute, and Fentress County high school. He has been a farmer, clerked in a wholesale and retail store in Chattanooga, and is now teaching school. Was licensed to teach in Morgan County in 1912.

MARQUIS LAFAYETTE GREER. 1878.

Parents: David A. and Malissie (Jennings) Greer.

Grandparents: Marquis Jennings and Ann (Crouch) Jennings and Samuel Greer, a well known minister of the M. E. Church and Chaplain in the Union Army during the Civil War.

He is related to Hon. John Jennings, lawyer and a prominent candidate for Attorney General, 1912.

M. L. Greer attended A. B. Wright Institute and began teaching in 1900, and has been teaching ever since. During the years 1911 and 1912 he taught at Wilder, and is now teaching at Allardt.

He is Deputy Register of the county, and works in the office when he is not teaching. He is also Secretary of the Workhouse Commission. He belongs to I. O. O. F., the Juniors and K. of P. He was married to Victoria Guffey in 1901, and resides in Jamestown.

JACOB W. MADEWELL.

J. W. is the son of Moses Robertson Madewell, was born in 1872 on the East Fork, was educated in the public schools of Fentress County and at Monroe Academy in Overton County.

He began teaching in 1902, and has taught at nearly every schoolhouse in the first district of the county. He has also taught in the fourth and sixth districts of the county.

He is a member of the Methodist Church. He was licensed to exort on the same day he was baptized into the church. He is now the pastor of Jamestown Mission, having twelve churches in his charge.

His father and mother are both living, and have always been highly respected by their neighbors. His father, Moses R., served several years as Justice of the Peace. For a long time he has been the miller at the old Bowden water mill near Boatland.

J. W's great-grandfather was an own cousin of James Robertson, the "Father of Middle Tennessee." His great-grandfather on his father's side was a native of Egypt and came to this country in 1795.

JAMES LAFAYETTE GARRETT. 1858.

Parents: Alex M. Garrett and Janette (Matheny) Garrett.
Grandparents: Elijah Garrett and Anna (Story) Garrett.
Grandparents: Samuel Matheny and Sytha (Grimsley) Matheny.

J. L. was born at Livingston in 1858. Moved with his parents to Fentress County in 1866, and has resided here ever since.

He obtained his education from the common schools and from Jamestown Academy. Has followed farming, teaching and the practice of law, and has served several times as Attorney General, pro tem. Has been an active minister in the Baptist Church for many years. He is now engaged in the mercantile business at Jamestown, Tennessee. He was County Court Clerk of the county four years, and Clerk and Master twelve years. Both these positions were filled with credit to himself and to the county. He is a democrat in politics. Married Miss Leeann Smith, November 25, 1877. He is a Royal Arch Mason.

ALEXANDER MARION GARRETT.

A. M. G., the father of J. L. G., was born May 4, 1829, in Overton, now Pickett, County, Tennessee. At the age of twenty-five he was married to Janette Matheny. There were twelve children born to them. Nine of them, six boys and three girls, are still living.

Prior to the Civil War he worked at the blacksmith trade at Livingston, Tennessee. During the war he moved with his family to Illinois. He returned to Tennessee in 1866 and located at Jamestown, where he worked at his old trade for a short time.

He soon took out law license, and soon had considerable practice in the courts. He did a great deal of work in the various county offices, especially in the Circuit Court Clerk's office. He was Deputy County Court Clerk for a number of years. In the latter part of the 70's he became a minister in the Baptist Church, and began to leave off the practice of law. He continued in the ministry as long as his health and strength permitted. He moved to Byrdtown in the 80's and served for a number of years as Justice of the Peace. He now lives three and one-half miles west of Byrdstown.

His grandfather was a native of Virginia. He came to Tennessee over a hundred years ago.

WILLIAM R. STORIE. 1891.

W. R. S. is a son of A. J. Storie and Martha (Greer) Storie, q. v., and a grandson of William Storie and Annie (Mullinix) Storie.

Maternal grandparents: Ben Greer and Talither (Peters) Greer.

Great-grandparents: Nathaniel Mullinix and Joshua Storie.

He was born near Little Crab in Fentress County, 1891. He was educated at A. B. Wright Institute, Fentress County high school and Valparaiso University. He received his first certificate to teach at Jamestown in 1908; taught in Pickett that year, the three years following in Morgan County and for the past two years has been principal of the Intermediate Department of the Fentress County High School.

WARD ROLAND CASE.

W. R. Case was born in Brown County, Ohio, in 1876. He came with his father to Rugby, Tennessee, in 1889, where his father, David R. Case, was employed as a teacher for a number of years.

Parents: D. R. Case and Frances (McBeth) Case.

Grandparents: Henry Butler Case and Mary (Lake) Case; James P. McBeth and Elizabeth (Spires) McBeth.

Father's ancestry were English-Dutch. His mother's were Scotch-German. W. R. Case's ancestors were among the first settlers on Staten Island in New York.

Mr. Case is well educated, and has acquired much of his education by home study. He owns one of the best libraries in the county and probably reads more than any other person in the county.

He learned shorthand at home and in the office of O. C. Conatser at Jamestown, and Ingersoll & Peyton at Knoxville,

Tennessee, and is a first-class stenographer. He was admitted to the bar in 1897 and formed a partnership with O. C. Conatser two years later, which partnership still exists. He with his partner have had an extensive practice in all the courts.

In 1911 he was appointed County Judge by Governor Hooper, and was elected to the position over an able competitor in 1912. His official books as judge of the county are models for neatness and accuracy, showing at a glance the condition of county affairs. Before his induction into office the county's financial condition was very much unsettled, owing to a lack of system upon the part of officials in keeping the financial accounts. His plan of requiring prompt and accurate settlements from all officials soon restored confidence and county warrants were soon selling at par.

His enforcement of the juvenile court law, and his efforts to acquaint the people with its wholesome provisions will be productive of lasting good.

He was chairman of the first County Board of Education in Fentress County, which did much to improve educational conditions in the county.

Member I. O. O. F., 32° Mason, Trinity Consistory, Nashville. Married Mollie Albertson, 1899, a daughter of I. D. Albertson, q. v.

WILLIAM A. BEATY. 1877.

Parents: James R. Beaty and Mary Jane (Greer) Beaty. Great-grandfather: Rev. Sam Greer, q. v.

Andrew Beaty, W. A.'s great-great-grandfather, fought at the battle of King's Mountain, and later drew a pension for his service in the Revolutionary War. William I., a brother of Andrew and a relative of Andrew Jackson, fought with Jackson in the battle of New Orleans, January 8, 1815. His great-grandfather Benjamin Davis was also an American soldier in the Revolution.

W. A. Beaty was educated at A. B. Wright Institute, American Temperance University, Harriman, Tennessee. He graduated at Draughon's Business College in 1910.

He taught several schools in Fentress, and two in Cumberland. He taught one year at Stoval, La., one at Boatner, La., and one at Wyatt, La. After completing the course in business college he taught one year in Draughon's Business College at Paducah, Ky., and was then transferred to Augusta, Ga.; after four months at this place he was made manager of Draughon's College at Biloxi, Miss. He resigned this position and came back to Fentress County and took charge of a farm he owned near Little Crab. He is now teaching in a school run by the Methodist Church at Baxter, Tenn.

He married Etta Stephens, a daughter of M. B. Stephens and a granddaughter of Zorel Stephens, one of the old settlers of Fentress County.

He is a democrat. A member of Lodge No. 614, F. & A. M., and Crossville Lodge No. 316, I. O. O. F. He is also a member of the M. E. Church, South.

CHARLEY M. HALL.

Parents: Luke Hall, Talitha J. (Atkinson) Hall.

Grandparents: David and Sarah Hall and Louis and Rachel Atkinson.

Great-grandfather: Luke Hall.

The Halls came from North Carolina, and the Atkinsons from Virginia, and are of English and French descent.

C. M. Hall was educated at A. B. Wright Institute, and at American Temperance University. Has taught school, and is now a member of the County High School Board of Fentress County. He has been married twice, first to Laura M. Lavender, 1894, second to Lottie Brown in 1908. He is a licensed minister of the Methodist Episcopal Church, and is a Mason and an Odd Fellow.

LUKE HALL, SR.

Luke Hall, the great-grandfather of C. M. Hall, was a man of great strength and courage, and a typical pioneer.

While living in Virginia, it is related of him that a man hearing of this rugged man, came some distance to the home of Hall, which was in Westmoreland County, Virginia, this being the same county in which George Washington was born. He told Hall that he had heard that he was a great fighter, and that he had come to try him. Of course Hall agreed. They walked out and rolled up their sleeves and began the test in the good old fashioned way. In a very short time Hall had whipped his adversary as usual, and after pouring water for each other to remove the blood, they parted friendly, both fully satisfied.

In those days "fist and skull" fighting was considered honorable, and was often indulged in for the amusement of spectators at gatherings. No unfairness was allowed, and it was regarded cowardly to use any weapon except the fist in settling personal differences.

MISS ADDIE TAYLOR. 1893.

Parents: P. A. and Armilda (Young) Taylor.

Grandparents: Joe C. Taylor and Mahala (Ward) Taylor, and W. D. and Nancy (Beaty) Young.

Her ancestors on both sides have been prominently identified with Fentress County ever since it was organized.

She was educated in the public schools, and the county high school, and has taught successfully for several years. Mt. Pleasant, Shirley and Allardt are among the places she has taught.

She is a professed Christian but not a member of any church. Her grandfather J. C. Taylor was a Methodist minister. Her mother's people are Baptist.

The Taylor family in Fentress County are related to Robert L. Taylor, the famous Tennessean.

MISS BERTHA WILLIAMS.

Miss Williams is the daughter of F. A. Williams, Circuit Court Clerk of Fentress County, 1908-1912; was educated in the public schools of the county and the county high school.

She began teaching in 1911 at Delk School, and has taught every year since.

She is a member of the Methodist Church.

Her father F. Asbury Williams is a prosperous farmer on Wolf River, and is an active worker in the Methodist Church.

He is a prominent republican leader, and deservedly popular among the people, having made an efficient clerk.

MISS MARY ROYSDEN.

Parents: Abe Roysden and Martelia (Pogue) Roysden.

Grandparents: Abe Roysden and Mary Roysden; Sol Pogue and Eliza (Grooms) Pogue.

Great-grandparents: John Grooms and Elizabeth (Apple) Grooms.

Miss Roysden is a native of Fentress County, the Pogues and Roysdens having come to this county and settled in the Wolf River region many years ago.

Her grandfather Abe Roysden was a teacher and a minister of the gospel in Virginia. He was of English and Irish descent. Her great-grandmother Elizabeth Apple was full blooded Dutch, and probably migrated from Pennsylvania to Virginia. The Pogues also originally came from Holland.

Miss Roysden was educated in the public schools of Fentress County and the county high school. She has taught for the past seven years at Pogue's, Roysden, Albertson, Clarkrange, Mt. Helen and Armathwaite.

She is a member of Rebekah Lodge, I. O. O. F.

W. ROSCOE BEATY. 1889.

Parents: Clemons Beaty. ———

Grandparents: Joshua Bowden and Polly Ann (Stephens) Bowden; David Beaty and Jane (Smith) Beaty.

Great-grandparent: David Beaty.

He attended the public schools and the county high school. Has taught successfully for three years. He is also a farmer. His family are of English and Irish descent, and a part of their family history is that they are related to John Smith, the leading character in the Jamestown, Virginia, colony.

MARION D. CLAIBORNE.

M. D. Claiborne is a native of Fentress County, and a son of Stephen Claiborne; a grandson of Dr. R. T. Claiborne, a recruiting officer in the Union Army in the Civil War, whose father, Leonard Claiborne, a college graduate, came from Virginia about 1830. He was of English descent. M. D. Claiborne's mother—Sarah Hayes Claiborne—was of French ancestry and a descendent of the French Acadians, who were taken from Nova Scotia and scattered among the English colonies in America, her ancestors having been brought to Louisiana. Her father was a native of Louisiana, and moved with his family to near Little Rock, Ark., and from there they came to Tennessee about 1867 and settled near Little Crab. Marion's mother was at this time about twelve or thirteen years old.

M. D. received his education from the public schools and the county high school. He has been teaching since 1908.

He is a republican and a member of the Methodist Church.

LEON CLAIBORNE.

Leon Claiborne is a brother of M. D. Claiborne, q. v.; was born in Fentress County, January 28, 1891; attended the public schools and the county high school; began teaching at the age of nineteen, and has taught four years.

He is a progressive republican. He is a member of the Baptist Church, and was licensed to preach in 1911.

JOE D. WARD.

J. D. Ward is a native of Fentress County and resides in the twelfth district.

Parents: James and Mary J. (Crabtree) Ward.

Grandparents: George and Lydia Ward; Isaac and Sarah Crabtree.

Attended A. B. Wright Institute, and became a teacher in 1907. Among the places he has taught are Tinch, Hood, Barger and Mt. Gilead. Has served as Secretary of the Republican County Executive Committee.

Became a member of the Methodist Church in 1910; is an active church and Sunday School worker. Has served as Steward, Trustee, Lay Delegate, etc., for his Church. Was County Chairman of the Sunday School Association for Fentress County, 1910.

THOMAS D. FLETCHER. 1880.

Parents: Jacob M. Fletcher and Martha Jane (Shilling) Fletcher. Thomas Fletcher, his great-great-grandfather, came from England to Virginia and died there. His father, Jacob M., came to Fentress County in 1865, and married Martha Jane Shilling of a pioneer Fentress County family. Thomas D. was born near Armathwaite, 1880. He attended the high school at Rugby and the Fentress County high school at Jamestown. He is a graduate of the Mountain City Business College of Chattanooga. He was awarded a gold medal for speed and accuracy on typewriter by this college. He is also a graduate of the Chattanooga College of Law, LL.B., class of 1913.

He taught eight terms in Fentress, four in Scott County. Kept books at Rugby and at Oneida. Served on the Finance Committee of Fentress County, 1911. Is now a lawyer and stenographer in Chattanooga.

He is a Mason, an Odd Fellow, Encampment and Rebekah, and also a member of the Knights of Pythias.

For many years he has been a cripple, and his success has been due entirely to his energy and determination to succeed. His perseverance and victory over the most adverse circumstances should furnish inspiration to other boys in Fentress County with more favorable opportunities.

WILLIAM PERRY LITTLE. 1871.

Parents: Vastine and Julia P. Little.

Grandparents: John and Elizabeth Little, and Robert S. and Amanda Little. The Windles and Littles were pioneer settlers in Overton County. Robert S. Windle was a leading lawyer at the Livingston bar for a number of years. He also practiced at Jamestown.

W. P. Little was born near Monroe in Overton County, where he resided until about fifteen years ago, when he came to Clarkrange in this county and began teaching there. He was soon elected County Superintendent of Fentress County and is now serving his sixth term. He received most of his education at Alpine Institute.

He is a great-great-grandson of John Sevier, and his great-grandmother, who was a daughter of John Sevier, is buried in Monroe, the old county seat of Overton County, when Fentress was a part of Overton. The Seviers entered several thousand acres of land in what is now Overton, Pickett and Clay counties.

Mr. Little is a 32° Scottish Rite Mason.

Married Pauline Peters, a daughter of W. H. Peters, Ex-Trustee of Fentress County, 1896. He is a democrat. Resides on his farm at Clarkrange.

VIRGIL H. PILE. 1870.

Parents: S. H. and Ermine (Miller) Pile.

Grandparents: Wm. Pile and Mary (Williams) Pile; Amp. Miller and ———

His ancestors were early settlers in the Wolf River region. His father was a well known and a well to do business man of the county. V. H. attended Hiawassee College and received a diploma from the business department. He has followed farming and stock raising all his life, and owns a fine farm on Wolf River and raises all kinds of live stock.

He was elected by the county court of the county to the office of County Trustee to succeed W. S. Smith 1911, and in August, 1912, was elected by a good majority over the nominee of the Republican primary, and was again re-elected in 1914 over one of the most popular men personally in the county.

He is a splendid collector, and is one trustee that has published regular reports of the county's financial condition. His business methods have endeared him to the people of the county and they feel safe with their money in his hands, hence his re-election in 1914 by an increased majority. He is the only democrat to hold the office of trustee since 1884, when Oliver P. Cooper was elected.

He was married to Nannie Williams, a daughter of E. J. and Susan Williams, in 1899.

ISAAC D. ALBERTSON.

Parents: John Albertson and Ruth (Dillon) Albertson.

Grandparents: Early Albertson and Elizabeth (Coulson) Albertson.

Early Albertson came from North Carolina and settled near what is now Gunter (P. O.) in Pickett County. His son John moved from there to Morgan County, and then back to Jamestown in 1827. There were only four other families living in what is now Jamestown at that time. They were John Conatser, Jesse Wood, John M. Clemons and possibly Marcia Millsaps and her husband Hiram Millsaps.

John Albertson lived in a log house located about where Frogge's store now stands, on west side of square. Albertson had to move out to allow court to be held. He made the molds for making the brick used in building the first courthouse. I. D. Albertson attended the famous Mt. Cumberland Academy in Poplar Cove and became a teacher. He followed farming and teaching. He was elected County Trustee in 1886. He was elected Circuit Court Clerk in 1888 and served eight years.

He was married to Ollie E. Jones of Kentucky in 1861. He died in 1900. He left a widow and four children, all married.

A. J. Albertson, a teacher, and Ben Albertson, an architect of Chattanooga, are his sons.

JOHN ALBERTSON, JR. 1827.

John Albertson, Jr., was a brother of I. D. Albertson, q. v. Came to Jamestown with his father when a few weeks old. The children of John M. Clemons, the brothers and sisters of "Mark Twain," were his playmates. He was fond of telling the story of Orion Clemons crying like his heart would break over a cup of milk he spilled upon the floor.

The first brick courthouse in Fentress County was built of brick made from moulds prepared by his father, John Albertson, Sr. The second courthouse, 1860, was built of brick from moulds he made himself.

He was a good citizen, was a farmer and blacksmith. Lived near Boatland and died there in 1903.

DANIEL VOILES. 1858.

He is the son of William Voiles who was a farmer and school teacher, who came from East Tennessee and settled in the old tenth district about sixty years ago. His mother, Elizabeth (Goddard) Voiles, was a native of Ohio. Daniel was born in the old twelfth district. During the war the family lived in the Poplar Cove. He was married to Lyda Hopkins, of Kentucky, in 1880. He was elected as a member of the first County Board of Education in Fentress, and was twice re-elected. While a member of the board he identified himself with every move for school improvement that was made by the board. Before the expiration of his third term he resigned to accept the position of Superintendent of the Poor. He has also served as Poor House Commissioner, and was constable in Tenth District for about ten years.

DAVID HUTCHINSON RANKIN.

D. H. Rankin was born in Kentucky in 1859. His parents were Thomas Rankin and Hannah (Shearer) Rankin; grandparents, Robert Rankin and Barbara (Hutchinson) Rankin; Daniel Shearer.

The Rankin family came from Scotland to America in the days of sail ships, and settled in Kentucky. The Hutchinsons also came from Scotland, the Shearers came from Germany.

D. H. Rankin came from Kentucky to Fentress County in 1880 and engaged in the mercantile and the milling business on Wolf River, and remained there for eight years, during which time he married Ermine Huff, a daughter of Alvin C. Huff of Pall Mall. In 1888 he moved to Jamestown and continued the mercantile business. At present he is also interested in the milling business.

MRS. MARTHA ELLEN (SMITH) MCDONALD. 1818.

Parents: Philip Smith (1769-1865) and Emily (Atkinson) Smith.

Grandparents: Owen Atkinson and Agnes (Goad) Atkinson, George Smith and Rebecca (Bowen) Smith.

Mrs. McDonald's mother came to Kentucky from West Virginia, then called New Virginia, at the age of twelve, her grandfather and grandmother George and Rebecca Smith having been killed the year before by the Indians. Rebecca Smith came from Ireland the year that Tennessee was settled (1769).

The famous preacher, "Raccoon" John Smith, who was associated with Alexander Campbell in the early history of the Campbellite Church, was an uncle of Mrs. McDonald.

Mrs. McDonald was born in Kentucky and came to Tennessee with her parents when she was eight years old and settled on Wolf River. She was married to William B. McDonald in 1839. He was of a pioneer Overton County family, his father having crossed the ocean when a boy and settled near old Monroe in Overton County. W. B. was a soldier in the Florida War in 1837; he was a double cousin of Judge A. O. W. Totten. He died in 1863.

Mrs. McDonald had ten brothers and two sisters, all of whom are dead. She has made four trips to the West to visit her sons in Nebraska. One of these trips was made at the age of 74, one at 86 and another at 90. She has eight sons. Mrs. Ben Moody, of Forbus, and Mrs. Lute Smith, at Jamestown, are her daughters.

She never attended a free school, but attended subscription schools. There were no free schools until long after she was married.

She has a wonderful memory and is well informed. She saw the Indians as they were being removed to lands west of the Mississippi. She remembers the Indian squaws as they passed by with their papooses strapped to their backs. She was then living near Albany, Kentucky.

REV. JEREMIAH M. STEWART. 1844.

Was born in Jackson County, Ala., and came to Blount County, Tennessee, in 1894. His grandfather Stewart came from Ireland and settled in Franklin County, in what is known as Stewart's Cove, and was there killed by the Indians during the Revolutionary War. Was licensed to preach in 1866. Did work as an evangelist in North Alabama for ten years. For the past two years he has been pastor of the Jamestown Mission of M. E. Church, South, having twelve churches in his charge.

Was a Union soldier during the war and served in First Regiment, Alabama Cavalry.

GEORGE W. CONATSER. 1840.

Parents: Philip and Peggy (Cooper) Conatser. Conatser's were of German descent, and the Cooper's Scotch-Irish.

His grandfather, John Palser Conatser, came to Watauga with Maj. Anderson, a great-grandfather of Judge C. E. Snodgrass, when Bean's cabin was the only house in the great Mississippi Valley. He moved from Watauga to Wayne County, Kentucky, and Philip Conatser moved from there, here, soon after Fentress County was organized. John Palser worked for General Greene about the time of the Revolution. He was a soldier at the battle of King's Mountain. The powder horn he used at this battle was presented to William McKinley while he was president of the United States, by G. W. Conatser. McKinley wrote him a nice letter, expressing his appreciation of the gift, and claimed he prized it more than anything else he had received, on account of its association with the great and decisive battle.

G. W. Conatser, or Uncle Hickory, as he is familiarly called, has served as Justice of the Peace, Sheriff eight years and as Deputy U. S. Marshal four years. In politics he is a republican. He is one of the best known men in the county, and knows everybody. He is a plain, old-fashioned citizen, and popular, and wields a wide influence among his friends. He owns a large farm in the Poplar Cove and lives upon it. A coal mine has been operated upon it for some years to supply local trade.

He was with Sherman in his march to the sea. Served in Company D, Second East Tennessee Infantry, joining in 1861, and was discharged November 6, 1865, at Knoxville.

DAN DAVIS.

Dan Davis, a farmer and slave trader before the war, was a citizen of the Poplar Grove until his death several years ago.

It is said that Mr. Davis lost a large amount of money at the breaking out of the war on account of his investments in the slave trade.

He was a distant cousin of President Jeff Davis and a relative of Hon. John M. Davis, of Wartburg. His father, Walter Davis, was a pioneer settler in Morgan County, and Wartburg was named for him.

WARREN E. TAYLOR. 1877.

Parents: James C. Taylor and Sybil C. (Northrup) Taylor.

Grandparents: Pleasant and Martha (Hamlet) Taylor; Niram Northrup and Mary Ett. (Buttoff) Northrup.

W. E. Taylor's grandparents came from North Carolina and were among the early settlers in the county. Pleasant Taylor lived for a long time on the Jamestown and Crossville road, three miles south of Jamestown. His home furnished many a weary traveler a comfortable stopping place. This road was much more traveled then than now. Many a drove of hogs, sheep and cattle have been driven by this place on their way to a southern market, before the railroads, and before the war.

He has been a farmer and contractor. For the past two years he has been Sheriff of Fentress County. He was re-elected August, 1914, by a majority of over 300, showing the estimation of the people of his record as Sheriff.

He is a member of the Masons and an Odd Fellow. He married Miss Dora Westfeldt, a native of Germany, in 1898. She came across the ocean to this country when she was three years old. Their daughter, Miss Ethel, received a teacher's certificate at the age of thirteen.

JAMES RAYMOND HOGUE. 1861.

Parents: Solomon and Caroline (Choate) Hogue.

Grandparents: Milburn and Rachel (Young) Hogue.

Great-grandparents: Anderson and Elizabeth Hogue; Dr. Thomas Choate ———

Great-grandparents, Anderson and Elizabeth Hogue, came from Virginia and settled at the foot of the mountain above the John Albertson farm near Boatland.

Attended schools taught by Anderson Hogue, Jr., A. J. Mace and G. W. Reagan. Followed farming and logging on the East Fork until about ten years ago, when he went West; is now farming near Colbert, Bryan County, Oklahoma.

His father, Solomon Hogue, was for several years a Justice of the Peace in the First District. He was killed in 1886, a saw-log rolling over him, where he was assisting in rolling logs into the East Fork River for rafting.

James Hogue was constable of first district one term. He was married in 1886 to Mary Jane Bowden, a daughter of W. B. Bowden, q. v.

David E. Hogue and A. M. Hogue are also sons of Solomon Hogue. They now live in Texas.

JAMES S. ROYSDEN. 1888.

J. S. Roysden is a brother of Mary Roysden, q. v. Was born near Pall Mall, 1888. Attended common schools and Cherry University. Taught several years in the north end of the county and two years in Kentucky. Taught at Davidson, 1913. Is a republican. Member F. & A. M., Lodge No. 281.

McPHERSON BUCK. 1873.

Parents: Claiborne P. and Sarah J. (Wilson) Buck.

Grandparents: —— Buck and Ruhana (Angel) Buck.

Born on Wolf River. Attended the common schools of Pickett and Fentress counties. Has taught at Fairview, Back Creek, Bucks, Broad-door, Dry Creek, Stockton and Grimsley, in Fentress, and at Gunter in Pickett County. He is a member of the Baptist Church, a Mason and an Odd Fellow.

JOE MULLINIX. 1872.

Son of John W. and Amanda (Choate) Mullinix.

Grandson of Nathan and Margret Mullinix and Thomas and Polly Choate. Attended Alpine Institute, and began teaching over twenty years ago, and has taught nearly every school in the first and sixth districts, and some in others.

Went to California in 1905 and remained one year; returned to Fentress County and married Nora Beaty in 1907.

He is a member of the Methodist Church. His father, John Mullinix, is an active worker in the M. E. Church, and for many years a class leader at the old chapel near Boatland, where he now resides. John Mullinix is a farmer and a member of the Masonic fraternity.

Joe is now farming. He owns the I. D. Albertson farm near mouth of Poplar Cove Creek, where he lives.

W. D. MULLINIX.

Parents: Isham and Vina (Boswell) Mullinix.

Grandparents: William Mullinix and ——— Boswell, his grandfather, who died on West Fork in Overton County many years ago.

He has followed farming and teaching, and for the past eighteen years he has been in the mercantile business.

He has held the offices of Justice of the Peace twelve years, constable and County Court Clerk eight years.

He was married in 1873 to Abagail Wood, who died in 1874. Married Mary Albertson in 1875; she died in 1881. In 1901 he married Amanda Shipworth, a great-great-granddaughter of Gov. John Sevier.

The Mullinixes came from North Carolina and settled in the Poplar Cove about 1835. Isham was a brother of Thannie Mullinix, q. v.

STEPHEN EDMUND FROGGE. 1865.

S. E. Frogge is a brother of C. C. Frogge, q. v., and was born on Wolf River. Educated in the common schools of the county.

He has followed farming, and for six years was a traveling salesman. For the past eighteen years he has been in the general merchandise business. Has at present a large store at Jamestown, and is in business with his brother-in-law W. E. Mullinix at Pall Mall, having a large stock of general merchandise at this place.

He was a member of County Board of Education for three years. Belongs to M. E. Church, and is an Odd Fellow and a Mason. He is a democrat.

Married in 1894 to Ella Pile, a daughter of Erasmus Pile, a prosperous merchant and farmer at Pall Mall.

His father, John W. Frogge, was Trustee of Fentress County for six years, and was a Justice of the Peace for years. He was also an attorney at the Jamestown bar.

EDMUND JASPER WRIGHT. 1865.

Parents: Joshua Foster Wright and Zibbie Angelina (Price) Wright.

Grandparents: Wilson L. Wright—died in 1895—and Hannah (Boswell) Wright; John Price and Sarah (Wright) Price, a sister of A. B. Wright and no relation to J. F. Wright.

Great-great-grandfather: Joshua F. Wright, who died soon after the Civil War.

Jasper, as E. J. is familiarly called, was born in the Poplar Cove in Fentress County. He was educated at Hiawassie College, Alpine Institute, and Grant University. He taught school for seven years. Bought live stock in Fentress and all the adjoining counties for a number of years, shipping them to northern markets. He now owns a fine farm and is interested in farming and stock raising. He also operates a general merchandise business at Jamestown.

He has served as Deputy Sheriff, and was Assistant County Superintendent for four years, and in 1885 held one of the first, if not the first, county institute for teachers ever held in the county.

He was elected Justice of the Peace in 1899, County Judge in 1901, and served until 1911, when he resigned. During his term as Judge the tax rate was lowered materially, it being $2.20 at the opening of his term. County claims increased in value more than 20 per cent before his term expired, notwithstanding the fact that the courthouse was burned and had to be rebuilt, and many of the county records had to be supplied.

He was married in 1893 to Alice Mace, a daughter of A. J. Mace, q. v. He is a Mason and an Odd Fellow, and has filled practically every position in both these lodges.

JOSHUA F. WRIGHT, SR.

Joshua Wright came with his family from Virginia and settled at Clarkrange, in the southern part of the county. He was probably the first settler in that region. He blazed out a way for the road from two miles south of Jamestown to the Bledsoe stand. He was a farmer and stockraiser.

He entered several large tracts of land in Overton and in Fentress counties. He is said to have controlled at one time over one hundred thousand acres of land.

He had two sons—Mich and Wilson L. Wright. The Wrights in Fentress County are generally the descendants of Wilson L. Wright, Mitcell's descendants having left the county.

WILSON L. WRIGHT.

Wilson L. Wright, son of J. F. Wright, was a native of Fentress County, and served as Sheriff, Trustee, Justice of the Peace and as County Judge. He was County Judge just after the war, when the second courthouse was built. His grandson, E. J. Wright, was County Judge at the time the third courthouse was erected.

Wilson L. was an office-holder in the county for forty-two years in succession. He rode to Jamestown on a side saddle to attend the sessions of the county court of which he was a member, when old and feeble and unable to ride otherwise.

He was the father of Maj. John C. Wright, q. v., J. Foster Wright, Jr., and Boswell F. Wright; and Jane Wright, who married Wash. Peavyhouse, and became the mother of Abe Peavyhouse, eight years Register of Fentress County, and John, Sam and Virgil Peavyhouse; Elizabeth Wright, who married John Conatser, their children were Pierce and Margret, who married Russ Choate. John Conatser died, and Elizabeth then married Thannie Mullinix. Their children were Vina, who is postmaster at Wilder; Marion, who lives in Washington, and Abagail, who married Hiram Pogue. Victoria Wright married Erasmus Pile, a merchant at Pall Mall, now deceased. Permelia married Benjamin Brannon, who was Sheriff of the county in reconstruction days.

Foster Wright died in 1900. He was the father of E. J. Wright, John Wright and Mack Wright.

Mack Wright taught school, served as Deputy County Court Clerk, and as Deputy Sheriff. He died in 1899.

JOHN C. WRIGHT.

Eldest son of Wilson L. Wright; was born in 1825. Became a major in the Ninth Tennessee Volunteer Cavalry, U. S. A., and served throughout the war.

Was a merchant at Jamestown for many years, and later engaged in farming on Wolf River and became one of the largest taxpayers in the county. He served the county as County Trustee. He married Mary Williams, and was the father of several children, all of whom became well-to-do citizens.

ELLEN WRIGHT.

She was a daughter of J. C. Wright, and was well educated. She taught school for several years. Was elected County Superintendent of Schools in 1895. She died before her term of office had expired, and her sister—Minnie Wright—was elected by the court to fill the unexpired term. They have the honor of being the only women who have held public office in Fentress County.

WM. L. WRIGHT. 1879.

Son of John C. Wright; was born at Pall Mall, 1879; was educated at American Temperance University and at Maryville College. He has taught school, acted as railroad agent, dealer in live stock, and is now president of the Bank of Jamestown. Is a large land owner—owns the famous Rock Castle region near Jamestown.

He was elected County Trustee in 1900 at the age of twenty-one, and was the youngest county officer ever elected in the county. He served six years. Before the close of his term of service, county claims were worth dollar for dollar for the first time since the war.

He is a Mason and an Odd Fellow. He is a prominent republican and has attended every republican state convention since he was twenty-one.

C. O. WRIGHT.

A son of J. C. Wright. Lives on the old Wright farm on Wolf River and is a prosperous farmer. He has served for several years as a member of the County High School Board.

WEBSTER WRIGHT.

Another son of J. C. Wright; was a teacher in Fentress County for several years. He now resides in Bellingham, Washington.

NOBLE WRIGHT.

Noble is the youngest son of J. C. Wright. He recently graduated in the Lebanon Law School and passed the State examination and received license to practice law.

JOHN SEYMOUR BOWDEN. 1870.

Attorney-at-law and stenographer. Born near Glenoby in 1870. Son of Joshua and Polly Ann Bowden, q. v. Educated at Hiawassee College. Has taught school, served as Deputy County Court Clerk, Deputy Clerk and Master, stenographer for Conatser & Case for a number of years, stenographer in the city government at St. Petersburg, Fla., one year (1913) while in Florida for the benefit of his wife's health. Is now assistant cashier of the Bank of Jamestown.

EUGENE M. SHELLEY. 1875.

Was born in Albany, Kentucky, in 1875; is the son of W. M. and Martha (Amy) Shelley. His father was a farmer.

E. M. Shelley has taught school, clerked in a store, clerked in a bank, cashier in Burnside Bank from 1900 to 1906; then organized the Weiser, Idaho, National Bank, and was cashier of this bank until 1909, when he resigned and came to Jamestown and bought an interest in the Bank of Jamestown, and has been cashier of this bank since that time.

Married Dora D. Harrison, a sister of Edgar Harrison, q. v., 1901. Is a member of Christian Church and an active Sunday School worker. Member of Knights of Pythias.

He was a captain in Company I, Fourth Kentucky Volunteer Infantry, in Spanish-American War.

B. DEAN BEATY. 1891.

A brother of D. O. Beaty, postmaster, Jamestown, q. v., was born in the Poplar Cove, where he now resides. Was educated at Pleasant Hill and at county high school. He has taught for six years. At present he is selling insurance for the Phoenix Mutual Life Insurance Company.

He is an Odd Fellow and belongs to the Methodist Church. Is a democrat.

MISS ELLA ANN YOUNG. 1890.

Parents: Alvin and Loretta (Pierce) Young.

Grandparents: W. D. and Nancy (Beaty) Young; Samuel B. and Mary Ann (Tompkins) Pierce, q. v.

Great-grandparents: John and Lovicie (Buck) Young, and William and —— (Morley) Tompkins.

Her great-great-grandfather Morley came from Ireland, and her great-great-grandmother from Holland to America.

Youngs came from Virginia in the time of the Revolutionary War and settled in East Tennessee.

W. D. Young came here when he was a year old with his parents. He was of German descent.

Her great-grandfather Beaty was a soldier in War of 1812. He was a relative of Andrew Jackson.

Miss Young was educated at Pleasant Hill and at the county high school, and has been teaching since 1910. Her sister, Nancy Young, is also a teacher.

She lives with her parents near Roslin. She is a member of F. E. C. U. 1536.

SAMUEL B. PIERCE.

S. B. Pierce, who resided, until his death a few years ago, in the east end of the county, near Armathwaite, was a soldier in Company D, Twelfth Kentucky Infantry, U. S. A., and took part in the battles of Chickamauga and Chattanooga, and others.

He was a Justice of the Peace for many years from the tenth district. He corresponded for many years for the county newspaper, and his letters were widely read and much enjoyed.

He was a Mason and a member of the Baptist Church. It is a part of the family history that he was a relative of President Franklin Pierce.

LEVI CALVIN HULL. 1849.

Is a son of Allen B. and Syrena (Mainord) Hull, and is a brother of William Hull, and an uncle of Congressman Cordell Hull. Is a prosperous farmer near Armathwaite.

He was married to Rebecca Ann Jones, daughter of Sam and Martha Jones, in 1874.

He is a democrat and a member of I. O. O. F. and a member of the United Baptist Church.

JOHN GENTRY. 1840.

Is a son of William and Sallie Gentry. His grandfather's name was also William Gentry, great-grandfather was David Gentry. The Gentrys came from South Carolina and settled on Wolf River in 1835, where John was born five years later.

He now lives a few miles southeast of Jamestown on Cumberland Mountain. He is a farmer. Was licensed to practice law in 1895. He taught school for many years in the county.

His great-grandfather, David Gentry, was an American soldier in the Revolution. His grandfather, William Gentry, was a soldier in the War of 1812.

FRED SMITH. 1890.

Was born near Clarkrange in 1890, where he now resides. Educated at Clarkrange and the county high school. Began teaching in 1910. He is a son of Alex Smith. His mother's maiden name was Lowe.

One of his maternal ancestors came across the ocean from Germany at the age of twelve and resided in New York when it was known as New Amsterdam and controlled by the Dutch.

Fred's great-grandfather, Micael Lowe, a tanner, was one of the first settlers of Knoxville, Tennessee, and was a renowned bear hunter.

P. E. JOHNSON.

Presley E. Johnson was born in 1843. He is of Scotch-Irish-German descent, but is a native born American.

John Sevier was a great-uncle of his grandmother on his mother's side.

He was educated at New Prospect Academy, Bradley County, Tennessee. Attended Medical College at Nashville in 1871. Came to Fentress County and began the practice of medicine in 1876. Moved to Rockwood, Tennessee, and retired from practice in 1906. Now lives at Rockwood.

He served three years in the Federal Army and now receives an age and service pension. He joined the Methodist Church in 1867, was licensed to preach in 1868, and ordained an elder at Cleveland, Tennessee, in 1872.

He married Nancy Poindexter in Bradley County in 1864 and has eight living children: O. W., Charles, Wayne J., Joseph N., Wheeler W., John L., Florence and Nancy.

All of his boys have served in the army except O. W., who is a teacher. Wheeler and John are now in the Philippines, where they have been since the time of the Spanish-American War.

Wayne J. Johnson is a merchant at Oakdale, Tennessee. Joe N. is County Superintendent of Schools in Morgan County. O. W. is principal of schools in Tyty, Georgia. These were all Fentress County boys and moved away from here about twenty years ago.

JOSEPH N. JOHNSON.

Joseph N. Johnson, a son of P. E. Johnson, was born in Fentress County, Tennessee, and lived near Boatland until about 1890 when he moved to Overton County. Has followed farming, teaching and is now County Superintendent of Schools in Morgan County. Was a soldier in the Spanish-American war and did service in Cuba and the Philippines. He was educated at the A. B. Wright Institute and at Athens University.

He married Orlena Frances Powell, a daughter of a prominent farmer in Morgan County in 1901. He is a member of the F. & A. M., Lodge No. 516, Sunbright, Tennessee, and lives near Oakdale, Tennessee.

GEORGE S. KINGTON.

George Strother Kington was born in Virginia in 1803 and came to Fentress County in 1840, and after four years went to Illinois. Returned to Fentress County about 1845. He was a soldier in the Florida War from 1835 to 1837. His father came to Tennessee from Virginia. They were of Irish descent.

He was elected Register of Fentress County in 1854 and held the office until his death in 1888, with the exception of four years when he was defeated by David Conatser, a brother of Hickory Conatser. He preserved the records of the different offices of the county during the war.

He lived on a farm which he opened up about a mile east of Jamestown, which is now grown up.

He married Harriet Bennett in East Tennessee about 1840. She was the daughter of John Haywood Bennett, a Presbyterian minister. In politics he was a democrat.

A. A. WILSON.

A. A. Wilson was born in Fentress County in 1881. His great-great-grandfather came from England. He received his education in the common schools, and by home study. He is a son of Eli G. Wilson and Sarah (Norris) Wilson. Grandparents: George Wilson and Sarah Pedew; James Norris and Mary A. Flowers.

He began teaching at the age of nineteen. Has taught at Dry Creek, Big Sandy, Poplar Cove, Upper Crab, Old Greer, East Fork, Little Crab, Campbell, Upper Indian Creek, Sharp Place in Fentress, and at Lower Harrison in Pickett County.

He is a republican and a member of the Baptist Church.

C. CLYDE MITCHELL.

Prof. Mitchell is a native Tennessean and was educated at Franklin County high school, 1906-1910; Winchester Normal

College, 1910-11; University of the South, 1912-13, and attended the Middle Tennessee Normal at Murfreesboro, Tenn., the summer of 1912 and spring and summer of 1913. Taught in the high school at Huntland, 1909-11, and at Cowan 1911-13. Member of the W. P. W. 303. Baptist. Democrat.

Married Miss Alberta Stafford, Decherd, Tenn., 1911. He was principal of the Fentress County high school, 1913-14.

JOHN R. HOGUE.

John R. Hogue was born 1862. He is a son of Vard Hogue and Catherine (Storie) Hogue.

Grandparents: Milburn Hogue and Rachel Hogue.

Great-great-grandparents: Anderson and Elizabeth Hogue.

He was born in Clinton County, Ky., and is of Scotch-Irish and German descent. He received a common school education; has taught school; has followed farming, logging, merchandising, and the practice of law. Is now County Judge of Overton County. Elected in 1910. Was elected to the House of Representatives, Fifty-fourth General Assembly, in 1904.

His father moved to Fentress County when he was a small boy and lived on a farm on the East Fork until 1905, when he died. John R. went to Overton County about 1881 and married Martha Sidwell, and has since resided in Overton County, and now lives near Livingston. He is an Odd Fellow. Has served as school director and as postmaster at Allons, Tenn.

Some time after his resignation as postmaster a draft in his favor of one cent was sent him, as a balance due in his postal account, by the United States.

ROSIER C. PILE.

Rosier C. Pile was born in 1877. He is a son of S. H. and Ermine (Miller) Pile.

Grandparents: Wm. Pile and Polly (Williams) Pile, and Wm. Miller and ———.

He is a native of Fentress County. Was educated at University of Harriman and at Maryville College. He is a farmer and general merchant at Pall Mall. Was Tax Assessor of the second district two years, and has been a Justice of the Peace eight years. Married Lucy Williams in 1903. She was a daughter of E. J. Williams and granddaughter of F. B. Williams, one of the oldest settlers of the county. R. C. belongs to the I. O. O. F., Lodge No. 283.

WADE HAMPTON ERWIN.

Wade H. Erwin was born January 9, 1819, on the Clinch River in Roane County, Tenn.

When a boy, in the bottoms along Clinch River, he was bitten by a copperhead snake, and when he was a young man blood poison set up from the bite and he had to have his leg amputated. He was so low at the time the doctors were afraid to put him to sleep, and men held him while Dr. Getts and two other doctors took off his leg.

It is not known where he acquired his education, but he must have had some, as he taught school. He came to Jamestown when a young man and began clerking in a store for Crosier. Later he became a partner of Crosier. Later bought out Crosier. At that time they dealt principally in pine tar, turpentine and venison. (See other sketch for further information.)

SOLOMON WYATT WINNINGHAM.

S. W. Winningham was born in 1859. He is a son of Henry Anderson Winningham and Martha (York) Winningham.

Grandparents: Solomon Winningham and ———— Winningham, and Jesse York and ———— (Young) York, a daughter of Billie Young of Scott County.

Great-grandparents: Billie Young and Richard Winningham.

S. W. was born in Overton County in 1859 and was raised in Jamestown. His father was a Union soldier in the Second Tennessee and died a prisoner on Bells Island.

The Winninghams were among the early settlers in the southeastern part of the county. Richard Winningham owned considerable land.

S. W. was Justice of the Peace six years, Town Marshal of Jamestown one year, in the days of saloons; Deputy Register some years under Pleas Phillips, Deputy Sheriff under W. S. Smith four years, Sheriff two years.

Married twice. First: Elvira Stepp, 1871; second: Mary Hix, 1891. He is a farmer and stock raiser and is now in the merchandise business at Shirley, Tenn.

JOHN BENTON BEATY.

John Benton Beaty was born in 1865. He has eight brothers as follows: Lewis, Prime, George W., James, Andrew, William, Green, Tom. Andrew is dead. He was Tax Assessor of the thirteenth district. Tom died when small. They are sons of John Beaty and Mahala Allred, daughter of Theophelus Allred. John Beaty was born about 1800 and died about 1868 or 1869.

They are grandsons of Col. Tom Beaty and Jane (Mullinix) Beaty, who was a daughter of Than Mullinix and an aunt of John Mullinix and Theophelus Allred ———— Elizabeth Allred.

Tom Beaty settled where his son, Hiram Beaty, now lives, and was a pioneer in the south end of the county. He owned a large tract of land. Andy Beaty, a brother of Tom Beaty, settled on an adjoining farm, where Abe Beaty lived until his death. Abe was Justice of the Peace for many years and died in 1911. These Beatys settled here about 1800, more than 100 years ago.

Tom Beaty was Sheriff of Fentress County before the war. Two children are still living—Tilda Stephens, widow of Sampson Stephens, a soldier in the Union army, and Hiram C. Beaty, ex-Sheriff and Justice of the Peace from the thirteenth district.

Prime Beaty lives near Little Crab and was constable for several years and a leading democrat of his district, and has attended many conventions, etc.

John Benton was Justice of the Peace for one term.

Prime, Lewis, George and John B. are Masons, and John Benton is also an Odd Fellow. Has been N. G. of Little Crab Lodge, I. O. O. F. Has held nearly all positions in Masonry.

All the boys are members of the M. E. Church and all democrats.

Theophelus Allred was a pioneer settler on head of West Fork in Overton County, and was the father of Anthony Center Looper Allred, a well known Baptist preacher, who lives on the East Fork in Fentress County.

WYLIE P. RAINS.

Wylie P. Rains is a son of William L. Rains and Elizabeth Clark.

Grandparents: Uriah Rains and Elizabeth Wells.

Great-grandparents: Levi Clark and Virginia Clark.

Grandparents came to Fentress County from North Carolina about 1836. Henderson Clark came from Ireland to North Carolina and then to Fentress County and settled on Wolf River in 1836.

It is a part of the family history that Henderson Clark and Capt. William Clark, of Virginia, who was later sent by Jefferson to explore the Louisiana Purchase, came from Ireland to America together and were of the same ancestry.

Wylie P. Rains was educated in the common schools and began teaching in 1892, and has taught in almost every district in the county. He served as Justice of the Peace from 1906 to 1912. Was one of the organizers of the Fentress County high school. Married ———, member of the ——— Church. Was elected Circuit Court Clerk of Fentress County in 1914 as the republican nominee.

JONATHAN SWAN WELCH.

Jonathan Swan Welch was born in 1847 near what is now Armathwaite. Helped to build Fellowship Church there. He now resides in Bevier, Mo.

His parents, Elijah and Catherine (Swan) Welch, came from North Carolina and settled at Armathwaite about 1830 on what is now Bud Hull farm. They were buried at Armathwaite.

J. S. Welch married Rebecca Voils, a sister of Daniel F. Voils, in 1871. Followed farming, mining and lumbering.

SHERWOOD DELK.

Sherwood Delk was born in 1824 in Scott County, Tennessee, and came to this county about seventy years ago with his mother and brothers who were: David, John, Henry and James, and settled on the middle fork of Wolf River. His parents were John Delk and Nina (Adkins) Delk. They came from Virginia to Scott County, where John Delk died.

His sister, Neva, married Hiram Crabtree, Sr., and was the mother of James Crabtree. Shookie married Rodney Pile, a grandson of Coonrod Pile. Edna married Hiram Crabtree, Jr.

Sherwood Delk married Malissa Helm about sixty-five years ago. She died about 1884.

MRS. HATTIE L. CASE.

Mrs. Case is a native of Ohio, and was educated at the Hammersville, Ohio, high school. Taught in the public schools of Ohio two years; eight years at Rugby, Tenn.; two years at New River, Tenn.; six years at Jacksboro, Tenn., one at Monterey, Tenn., three years at Oneida, Tenn., and four years in the Fentress County high school at Jamestown, Tenn., 1909-10-11-12 and 13, and is now teaching at Oneida, where she lives.

She was married to Prof. D. R. Case many years ago and has been associated with him in school work practically ever since, and is now teaching with him at Oneida.

ANDREW JACKSON STORIE.

Andrew J. Storie is a son of Wm. and Annie Storie. His grandparents were Joshua and Elizabeth (Reagan) Storie, Nathaniel and Betsy Mullinix. He received a common school education and taught school at Boatland in the old Chapel in 1879.

He went to Nevada in 1880 and to Washington, and returned to Tennessee in 1888 and engaged in farming. Married Martha N. Greer in 1889. He is a member of Lodge No. 614, F. and A. M., and belongs to M. E. Church.

His father, William Storie, was a second lieutenant in Eleventh Tennessee Cavalry, Union Army. Was wounded in East

Tennessee campaign; was captured and carried a prisoner to Annapolis, Maryland, and died there.

J. BATES CRAVENS.

J. B. Cravens was born in 1888. He is a son of W. J. and Belle (Green) Cravens, who was said to be related to Gen. Green. English and Irish descent.

J. B. received his education principally at the Fentress County high school. Began teaching in 1910; has taught at Fairview and Back Creek, and two years at Banner Springs, and is now teaching at Wilder, Tenn (1913).

Member Lodge No. 281, F. and A. M.

FREDERICK O. SANDERS.

F. O. Sanders was born in 1880, in Knox County, Tennessee. His father, James C., and his grandfather, William Sanders, were natives of Claiborne County, Tenn. His great-grandfather, Isaac Sanders, was born in North Carolina and was of Scotch-Irish descent. His grandmother belonged to the noted Evans family of Claiborne County. His maternal grandmother belonged to the well known Oliver family of Anderson County, and Oliver Springs was named for a great uncle. His mother was related to Henry Clay.

F. O. Sanders was raised on a farm; was educated at Carson and Newman College, S. N. University, Tennessee Normal College and the Southern Baptist Theological Seminary. He received B. S. degree at Tennessee Normal College in 1903. In the same year he was ordained a minister in the Baptist Church. He has been preaching and teaching continuously since. For several years he has been principal of the Stockton Valley Baptist Institute at Helena, Tenn.

STOCKTON VALLEY BAPTIST INSTITUTE.

This school was founded in 1909 by C. C. Choate and Rev. Wm. Louis Reagan, Andrew J. Smith being the first principal. For two years the school received some aid from the public school fund. In 1911 the Baptist Church took direct control of the school and it is now owned by them, and is operated under the supervision of the Home Mission Board of the Southern Baptist Convention, according to the plans, efforts and expectations of its founders.

At present (1914) it has one large school building completed, and also a dormitory of over twenty rooms. This school is located at Helena in Poplar Cove, not far from the site of the once noted Mount Cumberland Academy. The school bids fair to become a leading institution of learning in Fentress County, located as it is in a moral, well-to-do country neighborhood, where board and other expenses can always be had at reasonable rates.

CORDELL HULL.

Cordell Hull was born in 1871. He is the son of Wm. and Elizabeth (Riley) Hull. Both parents are from well-to-do families. His grandparents were Arthur B. Hull and Sirena (Mainord) Hull, who are the ancestors of the Hulls in Fentress County. He is at present Congressman from this, the Fourth Congressional District.

He was educated at Southern University at Bowling Green, Ky., and National Normal at Lebanon, Ohio, and graduated in law at Cumberland University at Lebanon, Tenn. He has followed farming, and has been very successful in the practice of law. He was a member of the lower house of the Tennessee Legislature for two years. Was Circuit Judge of the Fifth Judicial District for several years.

Was a soldier in Company "H", Fourth Regiment Tennessee Volunteer Infantry, during the Spanish-American War, with rank of Captain. He had under his command men from Fentress County. Among them were Sim Linder (died 1914), O. P. Stephens, Monroe Stephens, Fate York, D. M. Smith, Flem Boles, D. H. Beaty, John Beaty, Cullem Robertson and Wm. Stephens.

He is a K. P. and a democrat.

He has been on the Ways and Means Committee in Congress for many years. He drafted the Income Tax bill, and has had much to do with the present tariff legislation. His work on these two measures has made him a national reputation.

WILLIAM SHERMAN WINNINGHAM.

W. S. Winningham was born at Jamestown, Tenn., November 27, 1869. He is a half brother of Soloman Winningham.

He was educated at A. T. U. and began teaching when a mere boy. He was elected County Superintendent of Fentress County in 1891 and served two terms. He was married to Belle Hogue, a daughter of Vard Hogue, in 1890.

He died August 18, 1897.

HORACE VIRGIL WINNINGHAM.

H. V. Winningham was born in 1893 at Jamestown, and is the son of W. S. Winningham and Belle (Hogue) Winningham. He was educated in common schools of Fentress County and in the Fentress County high school. Began teaching in 1911 in Fentress County. Taught in Palma Sola, Fla., 1913-14. Taught again in Fentress County in the fall of 1914.

In politics he is a democrat.

ASA SMITH.

Asa Smith is a native of Fentress County. He was born in 1844, and is a son of Davy Smith and Fannie (Cobb) Smith.

Grandparents: Richard Smith and Jessie Cobb, a relative of Howell Cobb.

Richard Smith came from Virginia and settled on Indian Creek, at J. C. Smith place, and died about fifty years ago in Overton County.

Asa Smith has been a farmer all his life. Was elected County Road Superintendent at the April term of the county court, 1913. He is a republican.

He has had two sons to serve as County Superintendent of Schools in the county—David D. and James Smith. James is now County Trustee of Cumberland County and David D. is a prosperous farmer near Rockwood, Tenn.

BENJAMIN ANDERSON GREER.

B. A. Greer was born near Pall Mall on Wolf River in 1872. He is a son of David Greer and Malissa (Jennings) Greer.

Grandfather: Sam Greer.

Great-great-grandfather: David Greer.

His ancestors came to this county from Woodbury, in Cannon County, in 1855.

He was educated in the common schools. Taught from 1892 to 1906. Also a farmer. Has been County Court Clerk since 1906. Became a member of F. and A. M. at Byrdstown in 1894. Is a member of M. E. Church.

Married Paralee Guffy in 1895.

His grandmother was a Wright.

AUGUSTUS LOWDON. 1852-1915.

Augustus Lowdon was born in Ohio in 1852. His parents were of Dutch descent, and were natives of Pennsylvania, but removed to Ohio and came from Ohio to Fentress County, Tennessee, and settled about four miles south of Jamestown on Crossville Road about forty-six years ago. For the past thirty years A. Lowdon has resided in the twelfth district, where he was school director for many years.

He has followed farming and saw milling and grist milling. He married Mary Vanslyke in 1875.

His mother, Caroline Lowdon, was burned to death in a fire which consumed his residence and practically all its contents in January, 1913. She was ninety-one years old.

JOHN THOMAS WHEELER.

J. T. Wheeler was born in 1874. He is a son of J. D. Wheeler and E. E. (Holland) Wheeler.

Grandparents: John Wheeler and Jane (Igo) Wheeler and Thomas R. Holland and Sarah J. Holland.

Great-great-grandparents: John Igo and Elizabeth Igo.

He was born in Rhea County and educated in the public schools of that county and the Grandview High School.

Occupation, was a pharmacist for six years at Dayton, Spring City and Chattanooga. Admitted to the bar in 1901. To U. S. courts in 1903 at Nashville. Makes a specialty of land law and chancery practice.

He was Chairman of the County High School Board for five years. Is a member of the Christian Church and a 32° Mason, Scottish Rite, in Trinity Consistory at Nashville.

Married Margaret Lee Smith, eldest daughter of Hon. L. T. Smith. His maternal ancestors were English and Irish descent. The Wheelers and Igos came to Rhea County from Virginia and were among the first settlers.

It is a part of the family history that in the early settlement of America five brothers of the Wheeler family came to this country and landed in the east. One of the brothers went West, another—Joe Wheeler—came South, and the Wheelers in the South, including Gen. Joe Wheeler, were his descendants.

BERRY TIM GARRETT.

B. T. Garrett was born in 1874, in Fentress County, Tennessee. He is a son of Elijah and Cela J. (Rains) Garrett. He is a brother of Dr. I. L. Garrett. His father was a soldier in the Federal army during the war.

B. T. was educated in the common schools and by home study. Began teaching in 1899. Taught in the primary schools of Fentress County and one year in the Jamestown secondary school. Was assistant principal of the Stockton Valley Baptist Institute, 1909-10 and 11. He is a Seventh Day Adventist and a progressive republican.

CLAIBORNE BEATY.

C. Beaty was born in Fentress County on the East Fork in 1844. He is a son of David (Tinker) Beaty and Avy (Collier) Beaty. His father was a native of Fentress County. Was born at R. Smith Place. His mother was born in Overton County.

Grandparents: George Beaty and ———— (Wilson) Beaty. They came from North Carolina and settled on what is now Richard Smith's farm in early settlement of the county.

John Beaty, George Beaty and David Beaty were brothers and settled the W. B. Bowden farm. David Beaty lived on what is now Jerry Beaty farm, purchasing it from Wm. Crockett. All came from North Carolina at same time. David Collier, who lived in Overton County, the grandfather of C. Beaty, was a soldier in the War of 1812 and fought in the battle of New Orleans.

C. Beaty served as a member of the Lower House of the Tennessee Legislature from 1885 to 1887, representing Overton, Pickett, Fentress and Clay counties. John Gaudin, Pa——, and J. W. Giles, were candidates.

C. Beaty, Harve, James, Jones, Collier and Flem were all brothers. James and Claiborne were in the war, the others were too young.

Mr. Beaty has followed farming and logging all his life.

He married Dicy Beaty in 1867, and Levanna Stephens in 1892.

D. C. Beaty, who was Register of Fentress County for eight years, and now resides in Bellingham, Washington, is a son of C. Beaty.

David Beaty, George Beaty, the grandfather of C. Beaty, and John Beaty, three brothers, were the early settlers on the river between Boatland and Glenobey. They were all respected, well-to-do farmers. When the Beatys settled in this section there were plenty of bears, wolves, panthers, deer, turkey, squirrels, and abundance of fish of many kinds in the river.

WILLIAM CROCKETT.

William Crockett settled the Jerry Beaty farm across the river from Boatland. David Beaty bought his improvements and lived there over a hundred years ago. Crockett was an uncle of David, George and John Beaty, mentioned in the history of the Bowden family, and a great-great uncle of Hon. C. Beaty, and an uncle of the famous Davy Crockett. It is said that Davy Crockett spent a winter in a beech flat near Boatland on his way to West Tennessee.

G. W. SMITH.

G. W. Smith was born on Indian Creek in 1844. He is a son of George Smith, who was born in 1800 and died in 1888, and Peggy (McDonald) Smith.

Grandparents: Richard Smith and Ellen Smith.

Richard Smith came from Virginia and settled on Indian Creek. His father first settled in Overton County in what is called the Barrens. He later came to Fentress County.

Allen McDonald, the grandfather of G. W. Smith, was also a pioneer settler on Indian Creek. He came from North Carolina.

Old Uncle George Smith had several brothers. Andy lived in Kentucky; William and John lived in Overton County; David, George and Willis became citizens of Fentress County. James and George are the ancestors of most of the Smiths residing in this county at present. Wash, Allen, Richard and John C., are the sons of George Smith. All were well-to-do farmers. G. W. taught school one term just after the war. Was constable of first district three or four terms. Was Deputy Sheriff under G. W. Conatser (Hickory). Was County Trustee from 1889 to 1891 and served as Justice of the Peace from 1900 to 1912.

He is a member of the Christian Church.

He has owned and operated a farm since boyhood; also engaged in the mercantile business with his son-in-law James N. Franklin for several years at Glenobey and at Parkstown.

Harve Smith and John Allen Smith, farmers on the East Fork, are sons of Richard Smith; also George T. Smith, who lives at Jamestown.

George W. and Grant Smith, both of whom have taught school, are sons of J. C. Smith. They live on Indian Creek.

JOHN HICKS.

John Hicks was born in Fentress County, Tennessee, in 1843. He is a son of Joseph Hicks and Nancy (Downs) Hicks. Joseph Hicks was born in 1811 and died in 1898.

Paternal grandparents: John Hicks and Chrissie (Mills) Hicks.

Maternal grandparents: Wylie Downs and Chrissie (Nobles) Downs.

Joseph Hicks was born on Sulphur Creek nine miles east of Burksville, Ky.; came with his family to Fentress County in 1817, and settled in old twelfth district on Clear Fork on what is now known as Coonrod Pile place, which had been opened up at that time by Pile. Joseph entered a tract of land adjoining it and lived there until a short time before the war, when he moved over into Morgan County and died there during the war.

Joseph Hicks was a school teacher and was also a Justice of the Peace before the Civil War. The Hicks family have resided on Cumberland Mountain and all have followed farming and hunting for a living.

Wylie Downs came from North Carolina, and also settled in old twelfth. The Hicks were originally from the same county.

When the Hicks came to this county Marsha Millsaps and her husband lived in the only house in Jamestown. It stood on what is now the Yelton lot.

JAMES BLAINE REAGAN.

James B. Reagan is a son of Joel L. and Lucy C. Reagan. His paternal grandparents were John Reagan and Nancy (Finley) Reagan. Great-grandparents: Peter Reagan and Nancy Reagan. Maternal grandparents: Isaac Beaty and Susie (Green) Beaty. Great-grandparents: James Beaty and Mary (Smith) Beaty.

He is related to John H. Reagan, U. S. Senator from Texas. Attended rural schools, Byrdstown Academy, Pleasant Hill and Doyle College.

Has followed school teaching, traveling salesman, merchandising and farming. Has been a Justice of the Peace. Is now a rural route mail carrier and a member of the County High School Board. He is a Mason and I. O. O. F. He belongs to the Baptist Church and is a republican in politics.

Married Effie Chism, a daughter of Judge L. B. Chism, in 1907.

FRANK TINCH.

Frank Tinch was born in twelfth district, near where he now resides, in 1871. He is a son of Polk Tinch, a farmer, a saw mill owner and operator. His mother was Sarah A. (Northup) Tinch. He is a grandson of Anderson Tinch and Sarah (Spurlin) Tinch. Great-grandparents: George Tinch and

Frankie (Hicks) Tinch, and James Spurlin and ———
Great-great grandfather Tinch came from England to Virginia. George Tinch came from Virginia to Fentress County in 1828 and settled in the twelfth district, where his descendants now reside. George served in the Florida War with Andrew Jackson in 1817. He died in 1840 and was buried in Morgan County. He was a Justice of the Peace. His son Polk, and his grandson Frank, the subject of this sketch, have also held this position. Frank is now a Justice of the Peace. Polk served ten years, he also taught school and is now a prosperous Cumberland Mountain farmer. Frank Tinch served four years as Tax Collector in his district and one term as School Director. He married Rhoda Ann Blair in 1890. Member Christian Baptist Church. Republican.

ROBERT ANDERSON.

Robert Anderson was born in 1846. He is a son of Tom Anderson and Penny (Edwards) Anderson. Grandparents: Lewis Anderson and Sarah (Nobles) Anderson.

Lewis Anderson came with his family to Fentress County and settled on Crooked Creek on Cumberland Mountain about seventy-five years ago. He entered a thousand acres of land.

Lewis Anderson died about thirty years ago and Tom Anderson about sixteen years ago.

The Edwards family came from North Carolina about the same time the Andersons came. Riley Edwards, an uncle of Robert Anderson, also entered some tracts of land near the Andersons. He was killed by lightning, one of the Morgans was killed at the same time. Will Edwards, a brother of Riley Edwards, was killed on John Boles' porch by Ferguson's men during the war. James Edwards was a soldier in the Mexican War. About thirty Indians stayed all night with the Edwards family after they came to the county and ate about two bushels of meal made into mush and bread. They would not eat salted meat.

Robert Anderson is a farmer and lives at Banner Springs.

CLARK CHOATE.

Clark Choate was born in 1883. He is a son of Austin Choate and Martha (Hart) Choate. Grandparents: Austin Choate and Mary (Barnes) Choate. His great-grandfather was also Austin Choate. Maternal grandparents: Socrates Hart and Nancy (Brown) Hart, natives of Russell County, Kentucky.

He was educated at the A. B. Wright Institute and Union Seminary in Granger County. Began teaching in 1905, and has taught at Albertson, Jones, Buffalo Cove, Banner Springs, Mt. Gilead and Little Crab. He is a member of the I. O. O. F. and of the M. E. Church. Married Miss ———Reynolds in 1906.

DR. PHILLIP C. YORK.

Dr. York was born on Bills Creek in Fentress County in 1854. He is a son of Jeff York and Rhoda (Riddle) York. Grandparents: James York and Lucinda (McPherson) York. Great-grandfather: Phillip York. Jeff York and his father came from Virginia with Anderson Hogue to Knox County, Tennessee, and finally to Fentress County. Yorks settled on Bills Creek, entering three hundred acres of land.

James York was a soldier in the Mexican War. Phillip, the great-grandfather of P. C. York, emigrated from France. The Riddles were English. His mother was a native of Holland. Joe Riddle, an old Mexican and Union soldier who lives near Monterey, Tennessee, is an uncle of P. C. York.

P. C. began the practice of medicine in 1887. Entered the ministry in M. E. Church in 1885. Has filled prominent charges in both Holsten and Central Conferences. He had the Rockwood charge in 1908, Tracy City in 1907. He became a Mason in 1899, I. O. O. F. in 1901. He was a member of the County Board of Education, 1910-12. He died in 1914, was buried by the I. O. O. F.

SAMUEL ADKINS BERTRAM.

Sam A. Bertram was born in 1871. He is a son of Elza and Mary Jane Bertram.

Attended the Albany H. S. Has farmed. Began teaching about twenty years ago and has followed it as a profession and is now Principal of Sun Bright School, and is a very successful teacher. He taught for several years in this county and should have been kept here. Lack of appreciation of the services of good teachers and low wages have lost Fentress County many of her best teachers.

He is a Royal Arch Mason.

He married Electa Hancock in 1895.

Bertrams are of Teutonic origin with a mixture of French and Irish. William Bertram, his great-grandfather, lived originally in Bradley County, but moved to Sunny Brook, Ky., in 1815.

ABRAHAM ALEXANDER PEAVYHOUSE.

A. A. Peavyhouse is a son of G. W. Peavyhouse and Jane (Wright) Peavyhouse.

Grandparents: Geo. W. Peavyhouse and Rachel (Campbell) Peavyhouse, Wilson L. Wright and Hannah E. ———.

He is related to Col. Campbell of King Mountain fame. Has followed farming and teaching, and has served eight years as Register of Fentress County. Is now engaged in farming in Poplar Cove.

He is a member of the Baptist Church and is an Odd Fellow, Junior Order and a Mason. Has held the highest offices in both Odd Fellow and Masonic Lodges.

He was married to Susan Reagan in 1894.

STANLEY H. PEAVYHOUSE.

Stanley H. Peavyhouse was born in Fentress County in 1895. He is a son of A. A. Peavyhouse and Susan (Reagan) Peavyhouse. He attended the rural schools, the Jamestown High School and the Stockton Valley Baptist Institute. Began teaching at sixteen at Broad Door and taught two years there. He received a certificate to teach at the age of fourteen. He is now in Carson and Newman College at Jefferson City, Tenn.

GEORGE EDGAR HARRISON.

G. E. Harrison was born in 1875. He is a son of Benjamin Porter Harrison and Leeann (Noland) Harrison.

Grandparents: Benj. Harrison and Elizabeth Gunnels, Jesse Noland and Matilda Kendrick.

Grandparents were all native Virginians, and emigrated to Kentucky and Tennessee. His father was a soldier in Bledsoe's Company and made an honorable record. He is one of the six survivors of that company.

He followed merchandising eleven years at Albany, Ky.; dealt in real estate two years in Idaho and Oregon. Was director of the Weiser National Bank, Weiser, Idaho, and Western National Bank at Caldwell, Idaho. He is now vice president of the Bank of Jamestown, Jamestown, Tenn., and is also engaged in farming. He lives on, owns and operates a farm two miles east of Jamestown. He has a fine Cumberland Mountain farm. He harvested on his farm nearly 100 wagon loads of hay in 1913. He owns more than 13,000 acres of coal and other minerals, and also owns over 6,000 acres of timbered land in Fentress County. He is an enthusiastic real estate man, and is anxious to see this county developed. He has cut up several large tracts of land into smaller ones to encourage buyers to locate here and help develop the county.

He has been married twice. First to Miss Dora Emma Cosby, of Dixon, Ky., in 1899; second, to Miss Elsa Selma Gernt, of Allardt, Tenn., 1910.

He is a member of the Church of Christ and lives a model life.

GEORGE W. COOPER.

George W. Cooper was born in 1874. He is a son of David and Sarah D. Cooper.

Grandparents: Jacob and Catherine Cooper.

Great-grandfather: Thomas Cooper, a native of Pennsylvania.

Parents and grandparents were all natives of Fentress County. Thomas Cooper first settled on Rottens Fork of Wolf River, one of the first settlers there; then he moved to Indian Creek more than a 100 years ago. He was a teacher. He was a soldier in the War of 1812 and drew a pension. He rode horseback to Nashville to get his money.

Jacob Cooper was born and raised on Indian Creek. He married and reared a large family, all industrious farmers.

G. W. Cooper attended the Alpine Institute, and has taught in Fentress and Overton counties. He was a Justice of the Peace for several years, and was a member of the County High School Board. He was again elected Justice of the Peace in 1914 to fill out the unexpired term of J. B. Boles, deceased. He is a Scottish Rite Mason, a K. P., Odd Fellow and Junior Order.

Married in 1904 to Margaret Smith, a daughter of Allen Smith, an old and respected farmer of Indian Creek.

THURMAN PRICE.

Thurman Price was born in 1889. He is a son of Rev. Jasper Price of the Free Will Christian Baptist Church, and a grandson of James A. Price, a well-to-do farmer in the Linder Cove on East Fork. Thurman is a great-grandson of Nathaniel Price, whose parents and other members of the family were killed by the Indians. He came from Virginia to this county and became an early settler.

Thos. B. Price, a son of James B. Price, and an uncle of Thurman, was a soldier in the Cuban War, and is said to have been the only one in his company that always obeyed all the rules and regulations. James A. Price was a Union soldier in the Civil War.

Thurman Price became a member of the Baptist Church in 1903 and has been an active Sunday School worker ever since, and has filled every position in the Sunday School.

His ancestors on his father's side are Dutch, English and Irish, and on his mother's side, English and Cherokee Indian, Jarvis Green Adkins being one-half Cherokee.

RICHARD ANDERSON WINNINGHAM.

R. A. Winningham was born in 1837. He is a son of Richard and Polly (Hooser) Winningham. Richard was born in 1796 and died in 1893. His parents came from North Carolina about ninety years ago and settled on East Fork near the mouth of Cricket Creek and was one of the first settlers in that region. Settled on the Compton place, known also as the Joel

Beaty farm. Richard entered several tracts of land in the county. Adam Winningham, the brother of Richard, settled in Overton County at what is now Winningham Cross Roads. The Winninghams about *Wirmingham* are his descendants.

R. A. Winningham was a Union soldier, serving in Company "B", Second Tennessee, and did service at Fishing Creek and other minor engagements. Was captured at East Port and carried a prisoner to Chattanooga, then to Madison, Ga. Spent one night in Andersonville prison. Was then taken to Salisbury, N. C., where he and two comrades escaped by strategy. They burnt their faces, hands and arms with a hot iron and bathed in salt water and made the blisters white so as to resemble smallpox. They were taken out of prison to the hospital for treatment, where they escaped in the night. He reached his command again at Somerset, Ky., and rejoined them after being held eighteen months a prisoner. He was discharged at Knoxville, October 6, 1864. Now receives a pension.

He was with the Home Guard at Cave Springs in Overton County when that county was placed under military authorities to suppress the Ku Klux. Claib Beaty was commander.

He was constable of the sixth district of Overton County (Livingston) just after the war; was Deputy Marshal in 1868; was in a skirmish with the Confederates near Livingston in 1864, in which two of the Hammocks, James Ledbetter and another Confederate were killed. Two Union men were wounded. Sam Hooser was shot through the thigh.

BEN. R. STOCKTON.

Ben R. Stockton was born in 1843. He is a son of Isaac and Amanda (Randalls) Stockton.

Grandfather: Peter H. Stockton.

According to family history these Stocktons are related to Commodore Stockton and to the Stockton who signed the Declaration of Independence. Ancestors came from Virginia and were of Scottish descent.

Isaac Stockton came to Fentress County about 1840 and settled in Jamestown, and lived in what is now known as Erwin lot. He finally located seven miles east of Jamestown, where B. R. Stockton now lives.

B. R. married Paulina Shilling in 1877. His sons are J. K., a Justice of the Peace; Henry, a merchant, at Rugby, Tenn.; Grover, a lumber manufacturer; George, a contractor and builder in California; Henderson, a graduate of the law department of Southern University, ——, Cal., and resides in Los Angeles, Cal. His daughter, Stella, married W. R. Phillips, a well known citizen and prosperous farmer near Jamestown.

Mr. Stockton served in the Confederate army in Company "K", Sixty-ninth Arkansas Regiment, Infantry. Saw service in Arkansas, Missouri and Louisiana. Was in the battles of Jefferson City and Ironton. Served from 1862 to 1865.

Was Justice of the Peace for twelve years. Is a member of the M. E. Church, South, and is a democrat.

He owns a fine Cumberland Mountain farm and probably has more land under fence than any other farmer in the county.

AN INDIAN CAMP AND BURIAL GROUND.

On the B. R. Stockton farm there is a large rock house or bluff which appears to have been an Indian burying ground. The bones of probably a dozen skeletons have been uncovered in removing ashes from under the bluff to use as a fertilizer on the farm. Perhaps a thousand loads have already been hauled out and as many more yet remain. Five hundred loads were taken out before any bodies were found. Some arrow and spear heads, some vessels, some rocks for beating grain, acorns, etc., into meal, rocks for dressing hides and other relics have been found.

Some of these bodies were found in a sitting posture. Rocks were set up so as to form a box or vault about the bodies. From all appearances fires had been built in these vaults after the bodies had been placed there. Small sticks had been used. They were charred as if though the fire had been smothered out. This may have been done to assist in preserving the bodies, or it may have been used to torture them; again it may have been a religious rite the Indians performed with their dead. We are not sufficiently familiar with Indian customs to say what story these facts portray.

Several other bluffs on the farm have ashes under them and may contain bodies and Indian relics.

BIG AND LITTLE HARP.

There is an old Indian Trace that passes through this farm. It has been called the Harp Trace from the fact that the famous Harp brothers, who were robbers and murderers, traveled this Indian Trace when on their trips through the country from Cumberland Gap to Alabama. It is related that they were very cruel, and if stories about them are true there has never been a more heartless band than the Harps. They spared neither age nor sex in their cruelty.

According to information gathered principally from Mr. J. M. Fletcher (a former Justice of the Peace, teacher and school official of this county, now residing at Rugby, Tenn.), the Harps ranged through this county from Cumberland Gap and as far south as Alabama. They were originally from North Carolina, but were driven out of that State on account of their misdeeds.

At Cumberland Gap they had a dispute with a lady in regard to a board bill and a young man named Langford took the lady's part and got into a difficulty with them. But the matter was adjusted and all seemed reconciled. Langford left the home with the Harps and was never heard of again. He is supposed to have fallen a victim of their treachery.

The leaders were known as the Big Harp and the Little Harp. The Big Harp's real name was Micajah. The Little Harp's name is not known to the author.

Once it is said that a lady by the name of Stegall was preparing their dinner and left them in the room with her baby, which was helpless. She heard it crying, but it soon hushed. She supposed it had gone to sleep. After dinner, and after the Harps had gone, she went to her baby and found it dead. The Harps had murdered it.

The murder of the Stegall baby was the beginning of their end. They were followed by the father of the dead baby and other men of the neighborhood and soon overtaken, when both sides began shooting at each other. Finally the Big Harp was wounded and, not being able to stay on his horse, dismounted and wanted to surrender to a young man named Leper, or Lapeer, who, being better mounted than the others, had led the chase. Lapeer was afraid to go to him until the others came up. When Stegall came up he rushed right on and seized Big Harp by the hairs of the head and pulled him forward and cut through the back of his neck to the bone. Harp cursed him and called him a rough butcher and told him to cut on. Stegall did so and severed Harp's head from his body and carried it back in a sack and left his body to be cared for by the fowls of the air.

The Little Harp escaped the pursuers. They returned and camped out one night on their return and ate of roasting ears that had been carried in the sack and had been company to the head of the Big Harp on its last march.

The story goes that Little Harp, under an assumed name, later enlisted in the army and served under Andrew Jackson. A reward of $250 had been offered for his arrest, and some Alabama soldiers believing him to be Harp arrested him, and sent for some Tennessee soldiers who knew him to identify him. The Tennesseans agreed to disclaim any knowledge of him and did so, hoping to afterwards rearrest him and get the reward, but one of the Alabamians knew of a scar from a wound he had received in some of his fights, and when the was stripped the tell-tale scar was found that made the identification complete. Later he is said to have been executed.

For a long time afterwards parents used the story of the Harps to excite fear in their children to obtain obedience, just as thoughtless parents scare their children with stories of the Boogerman.

ALBERT L. BRIER.

Albert L. Brier is a son of A. L. Brier and ―― (Conatser) Brier.

Grandparents: B. L. Brier and John W. Gaudin.

He was born in Fentress County and moved to California several years ago. Was cashier of the California Moline Plow

Co., Stockton, Cal., for ten years. Is now secretary and treasurer of the Stockton Implement Co.

Was married December 10, 1904, to Edith P. Wood, of Nolton, Cal.

P. G. Stockton Lodge No. 11, I. O. O. F.; P. C. P. Encampment and P. C. Canton, Ridgely Lodge No. 15, I. O. O. F.

His grandfather, B. L. Brier, was a merchant at Jamestown for a long time, and owner of considerable real estate, and lived and died respected by all who knew him. His grandfather Gaudin was also a merchant and resided here. (See sketch elsewhere.)

His father, A. L. Brier, served as assistant cashier of the Bank of Jamestown for several years. He is one of the best business men in the county, and has worked on records in every public office in the county, and was elected County Register by one of the largest majorities ever given anyone in the county, receiving 1164 votes to his opponents 243. He is also a civil engineer, and has served at different times as County Surveyor.

H. C. Brier, a brother of Albert L. Brier, is a school teacher and is learning civil engineering. Bertha, a sister, is one of Fentress County's successful teachers.

PROF. D. R. CASE.

Prof. Case was born in Ohio in 1850, and was educated at the University of Lebanon, Ohio, graduating in the scientific and teachers' department. Taught for several years in Ohio, and came to Rugby, Tenn., in 1899 and taught there for eight years. Taught six years at Jacksboro, one in Monterey, five in Scott County, and four years at Jamestown as principal of the Fentress County high school. Is now principal of Oneida school in Scott County. His wife, Hattie L. Case, has assisted him in nearly all of these places.

He is a very successful teacher, is a thorough scholar, and is a student, and keeps abreast of all educational advancement.

He is a father of Ward R. Case, a leading lawyer of the Jamestown bar and at present County Judge of Fentress County.

JACOB WRIGHT, SR.

Jacob Wright was a son of David Wright who became one of the early settlers on Indian Creek, settling on the farm now known as the James Ecker Beaty farm. Jacob was a prosperous old-time farmer and lived to be nearly 100 years old. He died in 1913 near Boatland.

Jacob Wright had four brothers and two sisters. Their descendants live in the west side of Fentress County.

SIMEON HINDS.

Simeon Hinds is a son of Joel and Nina Hinds.

Grandparents: Eli and Sarah Mullinix.

The Hinds' came to Tennessee via Kentucky from Guilford County, N. C. He attended school at Cumberland Academy in Poplar Cove.

He was Deputy Sheriff of Fentress County two years and held the office of County Court Clerk two terms.

He accidentally shot himself with a shotgun while crossing a river in a canoe and died instantly.

His son, George Hinds, is a leading citizen in Pickett County, and was nominated by the republicans for Floterial Representative from Fentress, Pickett, Overton and Clay counties several years ago, but was defeated by the Hon. M. C. Sidwell.

PERRY HINDS, SR.

Perry Hinds was a brother of Simeon Hinds. Is a farmer and stock raiser in first district. Has held the office of Justice of the Peace and school director in his district several times.

He is a Mason and a democrat, and for many years a member of the Freewill Christian Church. Married Elizabeth Allred March 12, 1866. He owns and lives on the Elias Bowden farm near Boatland.

John I. D. Hinds (a son of John and Rhoda Hinds, and a grandson of Simeon and Elizabeth (Stone) Hinds, who later lived in Overton and were buried at Hillham), claims that the Hinds family are of Scotch-Irish and English descent. J. I. D.

Hinds is Professor of Chemistry in Cumberland University, Lebanon, Tenn.

John Hinds, a son of Perry Hinds, was a member of the first County Board of Education in Fentress County, and is the author of the plan (now in use in this county) to pay teachers according to grade, age and experience.

LOTTIE STEPHENS.

Lottie Stephens was born over eighty years ago in Fentress County. She is the widow of Zorel Stephens and the mother of Wade and Reece Stephens and Mrs. Matilda Cooper, all of whom reside in the Buffalo Cove near Glenobey.

Zorel Stephens once owned several large tracts of land.

Mrs. Stephens is one of the oldest persons in the Buffalo Cove and is loved and respected by all.

L. D. CULVER.

Dow Culver is a son of John and Nancy Culver. His mother lived to be about a hundred years old, and died near Boatland a few years ago.

L. D. worked in the tobacco business, buying and selling in western Kentucky, going each year until the Night Riders became so offensive that the business became uncertain and he has not returned for several years. Perhaps there is no other man in the county so well informed in regard to the care and culture of tobacco as he is. He is also an expert fisherman.

J. P. Culver, a brother of L. D., owned and operated until recently, the farm known as the Flowers place on East Fork. He sold it recently and bought a small place near the mouth of Poplar Cove Creek where he now lives. He has served as Deputy Sheriff and Tax Collector. The Culvers are noted for old time hospitality.

Tom Culver, a brother of J. P. and L. D., was killed in a skirmish between Beaty's men and a Confederate force under Colonel Hughes in Buffalo Cove in time of Civil War.

MAYNARD M. CULVER.

M. M. Culver is a nephew of Jake and Dow Culver, and is a school teacher and farmer. He has taught for over twenty years in the public schools of Fentress County. He has resided in the tenth district for several years, but now lives in Jamestown.

He married Martha Allred, a daughter of Rev. A. C. L. Allred, in 1893.

DOUGLAS WOOD.

Douglas V. Wood was born in 1859. He is a son of William and Elizabeth Jane (Smith) Wood. Grandparents: Mathew and Betsy Wood; great-grandparents: Jessie Wood and Noah Woolsey. He was born in Fentress County. Educated at Montvale Academy under Joe McMillin, a brother of Governor McMillin. Taught as principal of this school two years and also taught in Fentress County. Went to Waitsburg, Washington, in 1886 and began work as a farm hand, later studied law, became a real estate dealer and has become very prosperous. Is now a general selling agent for automobiles, and lives in Walla Walla, Washington. His father, William Wood, was a soldier in the Union Army during the war and died in the service.

WILLIAM W. WOOD.

W. W. Wood is a brother of D. V. Wood. Was born in Fentress County in 1862. Attended the Montvale Academy at Celina, Tennessee. Taught school in Fentress County for a number of years. Was elected Justice of the Peace of the first district in 1888 and re-elected in 1894 by a vote of over four to one for his opponent.

He owned and operated a good farm. Finally removed to Jamestown and engaged in mercantile business and real estate. About three years ago he went to Anadarko, Oklahoma, and is farming. He still owns valuable timber and coal land in Fentress County, and has also made large investments in land in Oklahoma.

MILLARD F. HURST.

M. F. Hurst has been a constable in the third district of Fentress County for several years, and has filled other official positions. He is a farmer and business man.

P. H. SMITH.

P. H. Smith is a son of Hon. L. T. Smith. He has been a Justice of the Peace for several years, and is one of the ablest members of the county court. Has served as County Surveyor.

He is an Odd Fellow and has filled with credit every elective position in his lodge.

Married Miss Buna Parmley in 19——.

J. N. SIMPSON.

J. N. Simpson was born on the northwest corner of the Public Square in Jamestown, Tenn., March 10, 1845. He is a son of William M. Simpson and Elizabeth (Rhea) Simpson.

His father was William M. Simpson, who came to Fentress County in the 30's and became a member of the Legislature.

William M. moved to Overton County before the war. After the war he moved to a farm on the line between White and Van Buren counties.

The following sketch is taken from the *Livingston Enterprise*, May, 1913:

"Captain J. N. Simpson was born March 1, 1845, in Jamestown, Tenn., being a son of William M. and Elizabeth Rhea Simpson. In 1853, at the sale of the landed estate of Job Carlock, his father purchased 600 acres of land on the West Fork River in the eastern part of this (Overton) County, at the price of $4,000, Jesse Roberts being his security on his purchase notes.

"In 1861 he enlisted in Captain Hutchison's Company, in which he served for some time as a Confederate soldier, but later on during the war he exchanged places with John A. Roberts, the father of Chancellor A. H. Roberts, of Livingston, who was at that time in Scott Bledsoe's Company, he going with Bledsoe and Roberts taking his place with Hutchison. He served in Company "I" of Paul Anderson's Fourth Tennessee Cavalry. Throughout the war he saw much and dangerous service.

"In the fall or winter of 1864 he was made a lieutenant and assigned to duty on Gen. George B. Dibrell's staff as Assistant Inspector General to W. P. Chapman, who was then Inspector General, and was one of the bravest soldiers this country furnished. He was one of the escorts of President Jefferson Davis from Raleigh, N. C., to Washington, Ga., where he surrendered in May, 1865. On coming back to Sparta with Gen. Dibrell he stopped at his home for some time. In the summer of 1865 Capt. Dowdy, a Federal captain, agreed that he would send him home to see his parents. He came to Livingston and there met Jesse Roberts, who was then a very old man, and was advised that it would be perilous for him to make a visit to the home of his parents. He acted upon this advice and went to the home of Thomas Moredock, where he remained until his mother could be sent for to visit him there.

"In 1866 he went to Waco, Texas, riding the same horse which he had brought out of the army. Upon reaching Texas he secured employment as a mule driver at $20 per month, hauling cotton to market. Later he went to Weatherford, and still later to Griffin, where he clerked in a store. By industry and economy he saved enough money to buy a stock of goods which, after a time, he traded for cattle, thus launching out into the cattle business. The plains of Texas then afforded excellent pasturage free. He saw the opportunity and seized it and was soon the owner of very large interests in the cattle business.

"In 1885 he first became interested in the banking business in Dallas, and from that time to the present has had more or less interest in the American Exchange National Bank of that city, being its president for a few years. At this time he is vice president of the Missouri, Kansas & Texas Railway Co. He is interested in farming on a large scale, and is prominent in business affairs in his home town.

"In 1875 he married in Weatherford, Texas, but his wife died in 1879, leaving one son—Sloan Simpson—who now lives in Dallas.

"He is a 32° Mason and an Elk.

"Is now vice president of the Texas Central & Wichita Falls & N. W. Railway, and is also vice president of the American Exchange National Bank, Dallas, Texas. This bank has a surplus of over a million dollars."

J. W. STORY.

J. W. Story was born in Fentress County. Graduated at Cumberland University in 1868. Practiced law at Lebanon, Tenn., then at Sherman, Texas, now at Forrest City, Ark.

Served in Bledsoe's Company during the war. Was lieutenant at the close of the war. Was promoted for gallantry by W. S. Bledsoe—has the original commission in his possession. Attended the Confederate reunion at Jacksonville, Fla., in a private car, where the author met him.

W. D. HULL.

W. D. Hull is a son of Louis and Matilda Hull.

Grandparents: A. B. and Syrena Hull.

L. A. Hull is a brother of Wm. and Lewis C. Hull and an uncle of Congressman Cordell Hull.

W. D. attended the A. B. Wright Institute, and began teaching in 1898. Has taught his home school seven years, and has taught several other schools. Was a member of the first County High School Board in the county and a member of the present board. Was Justice of the Peace for six years in the tenth district. Is a democrat. Married Josie Buck, a daughter of Landon and Margaret J. Buck, 1908. Lives on a farm near Shirley.

W. C. SMITH.

W. C. Smith is a son of L. T. Smith, a native of Fentress County. He served six years as Clerk and Master and one term as Floterial Representative for Fentress, Overton, Pickett and Clay counties, being elected as the democratic nominee in 1906. He is a regular practitioner at the Jamestown bar; does considerable work in chancery court.

W. J. SMITH.

W. J. Smith is a brother of L. T. Smith and a member of the Jamestown bar. Has served as Justice of the Peace, and has done considerable work in the various offices of the county.

MILTON H. SPURLIN.

M. H. Spurlin was born in the sixth district of the county. He is a son of Clinton Spurlin and Samantha (Stephens) Spurlin.

Grandfathers: Nathan Spurlin and John Stephens.

His grandfather, Nathan Spurlin, settled on Wolf River. His grandfather Stephens lived on East Fork of Obey, above the mouth of Piney, where John Stephens, Jr., now lives.

M. H. Spurlin married Lillie Franklin, a daughter of Hedley Franklin, a Union soldier in the Civil War. He has served as constable, Deputy Sheriff and Justice of the Peace. Was nominated in the republican primary, 1914, for Sheriff of Fentress County.

He is an Odd Fellow and K. P. Has filled every office in K. P. Lodge. Is a member of the Freewill Baptist Church. Resides at Wilder.

JOHN STEPHENS, SR.

John Stephens, Sr., was a brother of Isaiah Stephens; was a farmer on East Fork and a respected citizen of the county. He was a great deer hunter. His son, John Stephens, Jr., has served on the Advisory School Board for several years in sixth district.

Frank Stephens, another son, lives on the East Fork. He is a prosperous farmer and has held the office of school director and constable of his district.

THOMAS OWENS.

Thomas Owens resides in the twelfth district five miles south of Jamestown. For several years he served as school director of the twelfth district.

Elias Owens, a relative, was in Company "I", Fourth Tennessee Regiment, Bledsoe's Company, and was killed at the battle of New Hope, Ga., in 1864. Mr. Owens is a farmer. He is a democrat in politics.

D. L. RICHARDS.

D. L. Richards, who lives near Grimsley, is a son of John Richards. He has held the office of constable in his district, and has served a number of times as Deputy Sheriff. He is well known all over the county. He is a republican in politics.

A. J. MACE.

A. J. Mace served the county eight years as County Court Clerk, and was Sheriff two years. During this time there was a legalized saloon in Jamestown. He probably made more arrests than any other one Sheriff during one term.

For the past two years he has been clerk of the Advisory School Board in the third district of the county.

He has served on Finance Committee and performed various other duties in connection with county affairs.

He served in the Union army during the Civil War, although just a boy. He now receives a service pension from the government. He was one of the youngest soldiers in the service, being only about thirteen at the opening of the war.

BRUNO GERNT.

Mr. Gernt, who resides in Allardt, is a native of Germany, as is his wife. He is a naturalized American citizen.

He controls more land than any other man residing in the county. He is also engaged in the mercantile business at Wilder, Tenn. He has done much to develop the value of Cumberland Mountain land and to interest non-residents in securing homes here, and is always found at the front in every movement for the development and improvement of the county. He maintains a well equipped real estate office at Allardt, Tenn.

DR. PLEASANT HOGUE.

Pleasant Hogue is a son of Milburn and Rachel (Young) Hogue and was born in 1849 in Fentress County, where he resided until about twenty years ago. He followed farming, preaching and lecturing. He now resides near Pineknot, Ky., and owns a large farm. He is also engaged in the practice of medicine. His wife was Mary Ann Richards. He has a large family of children, all of whom are located on farms near him.

GILBERT H. BOLES.

Parents: James B. Boles, born October 13, 1856, died November 24, 1914; Zilpha (Albertson) Boles, born July 24, 1858.

Grandparents: Robert F. Boles, 2d Tenn. U. S. Vol., Civil War; Naoma (Worley) Boles; John C. Albertson, born April 12, 1827, died October 31, 1903; Cuzza (Beaty) Albertson, born August 25, 1830.

Great-grandparents: John Boles, with Capt. Beaty in Civil War, member of State Senate and member of House of Representatives; Matilda (Beaty) Boles; John Albertson, fifth settler in Jamestown, 1827, Justice of the Peace; Ruth (Dillon) Albertson.

Great-great-grandparents: James Boles, soldier in Revolutionary War, in battle of King's Mountain; Jennie (Franklin) Boles, related to Cherokee Indians; Early Albertson, soldier in Revolutionary War; Elizabeth (Coulson) Albertson.

Children of J. B. and Zilpha Boles—Gilbert H. Boles, born August 28, 1889; Herbert C. Boles, born January 18, 1892; Annie L. Boles, born June 29, 1896.

J. B. Boles, born on Big Piney Creek, near Wilder, Fentress County, Tennessee; removed with parents to Indiana during Civil War; attended school at Wayport and at Elletsville, Ind. After the war he came back to Big Piney Creek, remained there some time, then attended school at Joppa, Tenn., Alpine Academy and Montvale Academy. Taught first school at Boatland in the year 1881. Trustee of Fentress County one term (1896-97), defeating Calvin Tompkins. Defeated for re-election by James B. Reed. Elected Justice of the Peace in 1912. He remained in the teaching profession for more than thirty years. His last work was in school at Bills Creek during the fall of

J. B. BOLES

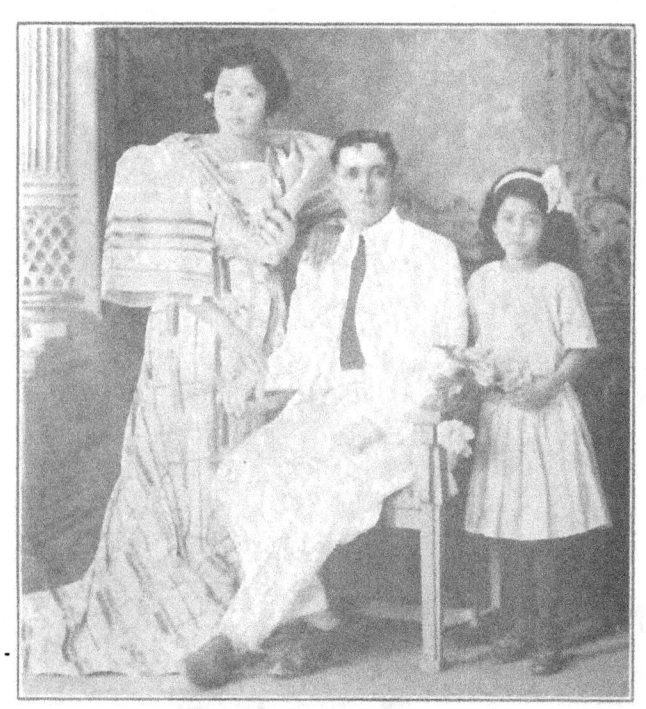

WHEELER W. JOHNSON
WITH NATIVE FILIPINO AND DAUGHTER

1914. He never joined any church denomination, but was a Christian. He was a strong believer in the immortality of man. Just before he died he said, "Immortal man shall not die."

Robert F. Boles served in 2d Tenn. Regt., U. S. Vol., Civil War. Was wounded in a bayonet charge near Big Creek Gap, Ky., a musket ball striking him in the knee as he jumped a fence while charging the enemy. Captured the Confederate commander after being disabled. Later was captured by the Confederates and taken to Bells Island, but escaped. After the war he spent the remainder of his life on Big Piney Creek. Died September 26, 1912.

John Boles, member of House of Representatives; member of Senate; with Captain Beaty during Civil War.

John Albertson, Sr., born in North Carolina, removed with parents to Kentucky when only three families lived south of the Cumberland River in Kentucky. Came to Tennessee and settled in Overton County, removed to Wartburg, Morgan County; removed to Jamestown in 1827, being the fifth settler in Jamestown; removed to Poplar Cove and spent remainder of life; died 1866.

James Boles, Sr., came from North Carolina and settled at Jonesboro, Tenn.; first child was born in the fort at Jonesboro. Soldier in Revolutionary War, fought at battle of King's Mountain. Came to Overton County and spent remainder of life.

Early Albertson came from North Carolina to Kentucky, being the third family to settle in Kentucky south of the Cumberland River, lived with other two families in block house for protection against Indians. Removed from Kentucky to Tennessee and settled in Overton County.

GILBERT BOLES. 1889.

Was born near Boatland where he now resides. He was a teacher for several years. Began merchandising about two years ago in partnership with Elbert Clark and is making the business a success. Has followed farming and is also a photographer.

LUTE SMITH.

Hon. L. T. Smith is a native of Kentucky. He came to Tennessee many years ago and engaged in farming and the practice of law. He has been in active practice for forty years, and is now a leading member of the Jamestown bar, and has a wide practice covering both criminal and chancery cases.

He represented his district in the State Senate in the 80's. He has probably drafted more legislation for his county than any other man now living. He is a democrat in politics.

ELBERT J. CLARK.

Parents: James Newton Clark and Nancy Jane (Albertson) Clark.

Grandparents: John C. and Cuzza (Beaty) Albertson; Jason S. and Jerusha (Saunders) Clark.

Great-grandparents: John and Ruth (Dillon) Albertson.

Great-great-grandparents: Early and Elizabeth (Coulson) Albertson.

Educated in county high school. Has followed farming and teaching. He is at present engaged in merchandising at Boatland in the firm of Boles & Clark. Has served as Deputy Sheriff of Fentress County.

Married in 1914 to Oakley May Beaty.

His father J. N. Clark is a teacher, and is also a photographer. He has two sisters who are teachers, Miss Metta and Miss Orpha, both of whom have taught in the county high school with success.

J. S. Clark was a soldier in the Union Army during the Civil War, being a volunteer. He served with Sherman in the Georgia campaign.

WILLIAM FRANKLIN BLEVINS.

Mr. Blevins, the mine foreman and weigh boss for Fentress Coal and Coke Co. at Wilder, is a native of Marion County, Tenn. Received his education from schools in Marion County, and in Dade County in Georgia. His father, Jonathan Blevins, a native of DeKalb County, Ala., was a soldier in the Civil War, serving in the Twelfth Alabama Vidette Cavalry and took part in engagements around Murfreesboro, Chattanooga and Stevenson, Ala.

He was married to Nervie Jane Derberry in 1894. Her father served in the Confederate Army during the war, and was severely wounded at the battle of Atlanta. In the retreat from Atlanta heard the crush of men's bones as the heavy artillery wagons rolled hastily over the bodies of the dead and wounded.

J. H. COMPTON.

Mr. Compton of Riverton has done more to advertise the mineral resources of Fentress County than probably any other man in the county. He owns or controls nearly all the land in the oil field of the county, and has been instrumental in nearly all the developments in this industry in this section.

He was spokesman for Fentress County at Chattanooga when the Dixie Highway was planned. His description of Fentress County, showing the great natural advantages of this section, was published on the front page of the Chattanooga News and attracted much attention.

ALBERT R. HOGUE. 1873.

Parents: Anderson Hogue, 1835-1887, Elizabeth Jane (Smith) Hogue, 1834-1913.

Grandparents: Milburn Hogue and Rachel (Young) Hogue, Owen Smith and Elvira (Stinson) Smith.

Great-grandparents: Anderson Hogue and Betty Hogue.

John Grant Smith, 1760-1863, and Sallie (Peyton) Smith and Billie Young and Louis C. Stinson.

Great-great-grandparents: John Owen Smith and Nellie (Grant) Smith.

Anderson Hogue, Jr., was a soldier in the Union Army during the Civil War, serving as a sergeant in Company M, First Regiment Alabama Cavalry Volunteers. According to the testimony of a comrade and messmate, "he was always at his post of duty".

John O. Smith was a soldier in the American Army during the Revolution, and was injured by a gunpowder explosion at the siege of Charleston.

The Hogues originally came from Virginia to Buncombe County, North Carolina, and from there Anderson Hogue came with others to Knox County and remained there a short while, coming then to Fentress and settled above Boatland in the early settlement of the county. Hogue brought his family with him in a wagon. They brought with them some apple trees, among them were the Red Horse apple, by some called the Hogue apple, from the fact that he brought the first ones to the county.

Grandmother Young came from Scott County, where her parents lived and was related to Judge D. K. Young. The Smiths lived originally in Virginia but were living near Charleston, S. C., when they emigrated to this county. Louis C. Stinson was a preacher. He came to Tennessee from Virginia, and later went to Evansville, Indiana, and died there in 1845. The Peytons were also native Virginians.

Owen Smith was living at the time of his death on what is known as the Owen Smith place, nine miles south of Jamestown, where he was engaged in the tar and turpentine business. He fell through the "hatch hole" of a steamboat and was killed. He was just leaving Nashville, where he had sold a load of products, when he saw a friend and started to shake hands with him when the accident occurred.

Elizabeth J. Smith had two brothers, Peyton and Hilary, in the Confederate Army, serving under Captain C. E. Myers. Peyton was killed at Clarksville during the war. Hilary died at Evansville, Indiana, since the war. Van B. Smith, the remaining brother, died at Booneville, Arkansas, 1911.

John Grant Smith died in 1863. His mother, Nellie Grant, was a relative of President U. S. Grant. John G. Smith took an active interest in General Grant's successes during the war, although over a hundred years old. Sallie Peyton was related to United States Senator Bailey Peyton.

Albert R. Hogue is a native of Fentress County. Received his education from Monroe Academy and Alpine Institute, began teaching at the age of seventeen, has taught continuously since in Georgia and Tennessee. Has served as High School Superintendent and County Superintendent of Schools for Overton County. Finance Commissioner of Fentress County in 1894; Notary Public in both Overton and Fentress counties; postmaster at Allons, Tenn., several years; has clerked in a store; conducted teachers' institutes; served on the Tennessee State Grading Committee, assisting in grading the papers of applicants for teachers' certificates from all over the State, July, 1914.

Received license to practice law in Justice's Court 1894, and in the Circuit and Chancery courts in 1895, in Federal Court 1910. Was sworn in to practice before the Supreme Court of the State, January 4, 1915.

Author of "Twenty-five lessons in Quick Figuring" and the School Improvement (Lodge) Club.

Milburn Hogue was a Justice of the Peace before the war, serving with Joshua Owens from the first district.

WILLIAM EDWARD MULLINIX.

Son of Winton Mullinix, a native of Pickett County. Followed teaching for a number of years. Is a graduate of a dental college. Was elected County Superintendent of Fentress County, 1911, defeated in 1913, again elected 1915. W. P. Little being a competitor each time.

W. E. married Delta Pile, a daughter of Erasmus Pile a well-to-do farmer and merchant, Pall Mall, Tennessee.

His father, Winton Mullinix, was a private soldier in Company D, First Tennessee Mtd. Infantry, under Captain Dowdy, enlisting at the age of eighteen.

STEPHEN LAKE.

Mr. Lake is postmaster at Allardt and is probably the oldest postmaster in the State. He performs his duty well. He is an active man, both physically and mentally.

He was a regular correspondent of the *Fentress County Gazette* until it suspended publication last fall. The editor made special mention in his last issue, regretting that he would have no more opportunity of publishing his letters. His articles, written over the *non de plume* of Mossback, were always interesting and worth reading.

MAX COLDITZ.

Mr. Colditz is a German by birth, but now a naturalized American citizen, full of industry and integrity. He is engaged in a general merchandise business at Allardt. He has served as Finance Commissioner of the county and is now a Notary Public. He is well educated and an experienced civil engineer.

LAKE BLEVINS.

Mr. Blevins has served the county for several years in the capacity of Superintendent of the Poor. During his administration the county erected a suitable building for the more perfect care of the unfortunate poor. The building is well lighted and ventilated. The plan was approved by the county physician, I. L. Garrett.

Mr. Blevins has two sons who are teachers—G. W. and A. J. Both received their education in the county high school.

MRS. ADA SUSSNER.

Daughter of W. D. Mullinix, q. v.; is a public school teacher, having been engaged in the work for many years.

Mr. Sussner, her husband, who died several years ago, was interested in the development of the Fentress County oil field.

W. J. TODD.

Mr. Todd, who was Justice of the Peace from the fourth district for some years, is a well-to-do farmer, and resides near Clarkrange. Elected member of Advisory Board of Education of the fourth district, August, 1914.

AZARIAH TODD.

Azariah Todd was a Justice of the Peace from the fourth district for many years. He made a reputation for his fearless and impartial manner of transacting public business. On one occasion a young man, who had lost two fingers by accident some years before, and was otherwise a stout, healthy young man, was before the court seeking to be released from road duty. While the roll was being called the magistrates examined the young man's hand. Mr. Todd was holding his hand when his name was called, inspecting it closely. He called out "No" in answer to his name, still holding the hand.

PLEASANT L. PHILLIPS.

Was a Mason and an Odd Fellow. Died 1911. Was for several years Register of Fentress County; also filled other official positions.

His son, W. A. Phillips, was a Justice of the Peace in the Jamestown district for a number of years.

Joseph C. Phillips was County Surveyor a number of times. He did a great deal of surveying for people in every part of the county.

W. R. Phillips, a son of W. A. Phillips, lives on the P. L. Phillips farm, three miles east of Jamestown, and is a prosperous farmer and business man. He is an Odd Fellow.

The Phillips' are all democrats.

JAMES GEORGE.

Mr. George came to Tennessee from the North and made this county his home for many years and became very popular. He was County Judge one or two terms. He finally moved to near Rugby, in Morgan County, and died there.

JOHN TURNER.

John Turner is a son of Micajah Turner, and is a native of Fentress County. He and his son, Oscar Turner, are engaged in the mercantile business at Manson, Tenn.

Mr. Turner was a soldier in the Union Army during the war

and receives a pension for service and disabilities of $100 a month. Not long after the war he lost his sight. He is a man of great industry and perseverence, and for several years after he became totally blind he followed farm work. It is said that he would go to the field and hunt up bushes by feeling for them, and grub them. Sometimes he would take a little boy with him to lead him from bush to bush.

J. C. BRADFORD.

Mr. Bradford resides near Allardt. He is a pioneer oil and real estate man in this county and has done a great deal toward interesting non-residents in making investments in land and minerals in this county.

R. H. RODGERS.

R. H. Rodgers is postmaster at Roslin; was postmaster at Tinch for eighteen years; a farmer and merchant. He is serving his second term as Justice of the Peace, representing the old ninth, fourth and fourteenth districts. He is a republican in politics. He is always found at the front in every move for improvement in the county. He is a relative of Judge Rodgers.

ENOCH B. JONES.

E. B. Jones is a native of the county, and is a son of Ervin Jones, who was a well known merchant and farmer in the ninth district of the county. E. B. was educated at the Alpine Institute. Was the republican nominee for trustee, 1912, but was defeated in the general election by V. H. Pile. His residence in the ninth district was destroyed by fire in the fall of 1912. He now resides in Cumberland County.

S. H. BEATY.

Shade, as he is familiarly called, was born on the East Fork on the old Wm. Crockett farm, owned by his father, Jeremiah Beaty. He is a farmer and business man and well informed in Fentress County affairs. He lives near Banner Springs. His brother, Putnam Beaty, and his brother-in-law, Harry

Davis, live on the old homestead on the East Fork opposite Boatland.

C. K. McBROOM.

Mr. McBroom is a native of Putnam County. He came to this county twelve or fifteen years ago and engaged in the mercantile business at Wilder, at the same time reading and practicing law, having been admitted to the bar at Cookeville.

He sold out at Wilder seven or eight years ago and came to Jamestown and began the practice of law here. He also gave some attention to farming. He was appointed Clerk and Master in 1912 by Judge A. H. Roberts and is the present incumbent.

JUDGE ALBERT H. ROBERTS.

Parents: J. A. and Sarah E. (Carlock) Roberts.

Grandparents: Jesse and Mahala (Murdock) Roberts, and B. L. and Eliza (Hayter) Carlock.

Graduated at Hiawassee College, A. B., 1889; A. M., 1892. Taught for several years at Alpine Institute. Quit teaching and began the practice of law, and soon became a leader at the bar in Overton, Fentress and adjoining counties. He was elected Chancellor of Fourth Division, 1910, defeating the Hon. L. D. Hill in democratic primary and Hon. J. W. Dorton, the republican nominee, in the regular election.

Upon his election it was found that he was incompetent in more than half the cases on the docket in two counties of the division by reason of having been counsel in that per cent of the cases on the docket. In Fentress County he was counsel in more than sixty cases out of about 105.

Jesse Roberts was a wealthy slave owner before the Civil War. J. A. Roberts was a soldier in the Confederate army.

JUDGE CHARLES EDWARD SNODGRASS.

Parents: Thos. and Eliza Jane (Evans) Snodgrass.

Grandparents: David and Mary (Johnson) Snodgrass; Sevier and Nancy (Rotan) Evans.

He was born in White County in 1866. Studied law in the office of his uncle, H. C. Snodgrass. Began the practice of law at Crossville in partnership with his father and his uncle. They all attended the courts at Jamestown and did a good practice here. C. E. Snodgrass was at one time a partner with Evans & Roberts at this place.

He was a member of the fifty-sixth and fifty-seven Congress from the Fourth Congressional District. In 1906 he became Judge of the Fifth Judicial Circuit by appointment from Gov. Cox and has been twice elected to the position since his appointment, and is the present incumbent.

ATTORNEY GENERAL W. H. BUTTRAM.

He is a son of John and Mary (Hurt) Buttram. His father was a sergeant in the Seventh Tennessee Mounted Infantry, U. S. A., in the Civil War. General Buttram was partly educated at Oak Hill, in Overton County. His struggle for an education over the most unfavorable circumstances attracted the attention of all who knew him. He is a great favorite among the common people of his district, as evidenced by the large vote accorded him when he was first elected Attorney General in 1902, and when he was re-elected in 1910.

He was a delegate to the National Republican Convention that nominated Taft in 1908. He is prominent in all the councils of his party in East Tennessee.

JESSE FRANKLIN.

Parents: George W. and Dicey (Smith) Franklin, both of whom died during the war.

Jesse was born in Fentress County, but now resides in Pickett County. Has followed farming, merchandising and banking. Is now interested in Otto Mercantile Co., and is assistant cashier of Pickett County Bank & Trust Co.

Married Sibby J. Smith, 1876. Member I. O. O. F. and F. & A. M. Member of Christian Church.

WILLIAM DUDLEY WRIGHT.

Parents: A. B. and Cynthia (Frogge) Wright.

Grandparents: John W. and Perina (Dale) Wright, and John W. and Rachel (Carpenter) Frogge.

His father, A. B. Wright, was a famous Methodist preacher in this and adjoining counties, and was unusually popular. He was the founder of the splendid school at Burrville in Morgan County, now known as the A. B. Wright Institute. He was for many years a county official in Fentress County, serving as County Court Clerk and in other positions.

From 1888 to 1893 W. D. Wright was Clerk and Master in Morgan County. Served as United States District Attorney, 1897-1906. Elected Chancellor for Chancery Division of Knox County, 1910. Resides in Knoxville.

THOMAS ASBURY WRIGHT.

He is a brother of Judge W. D. Wright. He is also a native of Fentress County. He has a wide reputation as a lawyer, and has been much talked of in connection with the republican nomination for Governor of Tennessee. He is a prominent republican leader in all the councils of the party.

O. P. PILE. 1874.

Parents: Stephen H. and Ermine (Miller) Pile.

Grandparents: William and Pollie (Williams) Pile, and Armstead and Tennessee (McGhee) Miller.

Graduated at Hiawassee College, 1893. He has followed farming, lumbering and merchandising. From 1901 to 1908 he followed civil engineering, working for Fentress Coal & Coke Co. Since 1908 he has been the chief engineer for Davidson, Hicks & Greene Co. He surveyed the line for the Highland Railway from Wilder to Cook Place for them. This company is engaged in lumbering and owns a large boundary of land in the western part of Fentress. Most of the timber is drawn to the top of the mountain by machinery, and then hauled on tramways to their main railway line, which is a standard gauge road. They have done an enormous business in this county in the past six years.

Mr. Pile has served as a Justice of the Peace from the Wilder district. He was nominated by the Democrats for Senator from the Tenth Senatorial District August 27, 1914.

JASON L. PILE.

Jason is a brother of O. P. and V. H. Pile. Is a successful farmer. Owns a farm on Wolf River, where he resides. He has been a member of the County High School Board for several years, and is a good school man. Belongs to Jamestown I. O. O. F.

ORION CLEMONS CONATSER.

Was born at Jamestown in 1863. Graduated at Hiawassee College, 1883. Attended the Cumberland University, at Lebanon, and graduated there in 1885, receiving the degree of B.L.

He worked on a farm and taught school for the money to pay his way in the law school. He is an able lawyer and has a wide practice, maintaining offices at Harriman, Jamestown and Livingston. Resides at Harriman.

He served several years as County Attorney of Fentress County, and Clerk and Master from 1888 to 1894.

Member F. & A. M., Cookeville Chapter 112, R. A. M.; Chevalier Commandery K. T., Trinity Consistory No. 2; 32°, Nashville. I. O. O. F., No. 179, Cookeville. In politics, republican.

PORTER SEYMOUR WOOD. 1875-1913.

Parents: Jerry and Jane (Harmon) Wood.

Grandparents: Mathew and Betsy (Woolsey) Wood, and John and Margret (Ramsey) Harmon.

Jerry Wood was a farmer, and a very successful merchant at Boatland. He was also postmaster for many years.

P. S. Wood followed farming and merchandising. Had been in the latter business about fifteen years. He was thrown from his horse and killed near his home, 1913.

He married Hattie Roberts, a daughter of George Roberts, of Eagle Creek, in Overton County, and a granddaughter of Jesse Roberts, in 1897.

He was a Mason and an Odd Fellow.

JAMES B. REED.

Mr. Reed is a native of Fentress County and has served it in various capacities. He was Trustee for four years and Sheriff perhaps two terms. He now resides at Monroe, Tenn.

ALONZO REED.

Alonzo Reed has served for years as Deputy Sheriff. He is a farmer and resides on Wolf River.

WILLIAM PILE.

Mr. Pile is a son of S. H. and Ermine Pile, and lives on Wolf River, and is engaged in the milling business, operating a roller mill on Wolf River.

HENRY POTTER.

Mr. Potter is a farmer near Lake, in the eastern part of the county. His son, Thomas Potter, is in the United States army, and has been stationed near the Mexican border for the past two years. His sons—Cordell and Bryan, and his daughter, Ibidell—are teachers.

JOE UPCHURCH.

Joe Upchurch is a native of Fentress County, and is a Wolf River farmer. He has served the county as Circuit Court Clerk and in other minor positions. Is now a member of the Advisory Board of Education of his district.

NELSON WRIGHT.

Mr. Wright is a farmer and business man on Indian Creek. He was in the mercantile business at Manson for several years, under the firm name of Turner & Wright; sold out to Mr. Turner about two years ago. He is now a member of the County Board of Education from the third district.

GEORGE W. REAGAN.

G. W. Reagan has been in the mercantile business in the Poplar Cove for a number of years. He has also been in the logging business on East Fork for several years.

WILLIAM A. GARRETT.

W. A. Garrett is the son of Rev. J. L. and Leeann (Smith) Garrett. W. A. has been practicing law in Fentress and Pickett counties for many years.

He has served the county as Finance Commissioner, Notary Public, and is the present County Surveyor.

ROSCOE D. HOGUE. 1895.

R. D. Hogue is the son of Albert R. Hogue and Matilda (Hinds) Hogue, and a grandson of Perry Hinds, Sr., q. v. Born in Overton County, near Alltens.

He received teachers' license at the age of fourteen, and secondary school diploma at sixteen. Taught at Hood School 1912 and 1913, and at Allons, Tenn., in Overton County, January and February, 1914. He began teaching at Munson, Florida, September, 1914.

He attended high school at Finleyson, Georgia, and the Fentress County high school at Jamestown, Tenn.

J. A. HOGUE.

Son of Vard and Catherine (Story) Hogue, and a brother of Judge John R. Hogue, of Overton County. Is a native of Fentress, but has resided in Texas and in Georgia. Has followed farming. Now lives on the old home place, where his great-grandfather and great-grandmother Hogue are buried, on the East Fork.

SAM WILLIAMS.

Sam is the son of A. B. Williams, and lives on Wolf River, and is engaged in farming. He is now serving as Justice of the Peace from the new second district.

W. J. BLEVINS.

Mr. Blevins, the present County Court Clerk, was elected to the office August 6, 1914, by a majority of 326 votes. He resided at the time of his election near Armathwaite, and was engaged in farming.

CALVIN J. TOMPKINS.

Uncle Cal, as he is familiarly called, lives in the old tenth district, near Mt. Helen, and is an influential republican leader in that section. He has held several minor district offices; is now a member of the Advisory School Board. He is a farmer.

INDEX

OLD TEACHERS, FENTRESS COUNTY

Back row, from the left: 1. J. S. Roysden; 2. Mark Greer; 3. M. F. Buck; 4. J. B. Boles; 5. A. A. Wilson; 6. A. R. Hogue; 7. W. A. Beaty; 8. W. P. Little; 9. M. M. Culver; 10. Wiley P. Rains; 11. Rev. C. C. Frogge.

Front row: 1. Rev. J. W. Madewell; 2. W. D. Hull; 3. James P. Buck; 4. Benj. T. Garrett; 5. J. N. Clark; 6. Mrs. Ada Sussner; 7. Miss Alice Campbell; 8. Mrs. W. P. Little; 9. Joe Mullinix.

GROUP OF YOUNG TEACHERS

Back row, from the left: 1 ——————; 2. Stanley Hull; 3. Miss Forest Conatser; 4. Virgil Winningham; 5. Travis Evans; 6. Mrs. W. R. Storie; 7. Fred Smith; 8. W. R. Beaty; 9. A. J. Blevins.

Second row: 1. O. O. Frogge; 2. Miss Rains; 3. Miss Gertie Blevins; 4. Miss Bertha Williams; 5. Miss Vina Stephens; 6. O. O. Greer; 7. Miss Laura Wood; 8. ——————; 9. Miss Ella Young; 10. ——————.

Third row: 1. Cordell Potter; 2. ——————; 3. G. W. Blevins; 4. Neely Evans; 5. Tim Campbell; 6. Miss Lora Coakley; 7. —— Smith; 8. Miss Cora Stewart; 9. Miss Metta Clark.

Front row: 1. Herbert Boles; 2. Miss Orpha Clark; 3. R. D. Hogue.

COUNTY OFFICIALS OF FENTRESS COUNTY, 1912-14

From left. Back row: 1. J. K. Stockton, J. P.; 2. V. H. Pile, Trustee; 3. Asa Smith, Road Superintendent; 4. G. W. Conatser, Coroner; 5. O. P. Pile, J. P.; 6. Sam Williams, J. P.; 7. A. J. Storie; 8. W. R. Case, County Judge; 9. John Gentry; 10. J. Norman, J. P.; 11. M. F. Spurling, J. P.

Second row: 1. M. F. Hurst, Constable; 2. Dillard Wright, J. P.; 3. A. A. Peavyhouse, Register; 4. R. H. Rodgers, J. P.; 5. D. O. Beaty, Deputy Clerk and Master; 6. B. A. Greer, County Court Clerk; 7. J. W. Evans, County Attorney; 8. Frank Tinch, J. P.; 9. Mark Greer, Deputy Register.

Front row: 1. James B. Boles, J. P.; 2. Pat. H. Smith, J. P.; 3. J. B. Reagan, J. P.; 4. Comer K. McBroom, Clerk and Master; 5. L. C. Hull; 6. Rosier C. Pile, J. P.; 7. F. A. Williams, Circuit Court Clerk; 8. W. A. Garrett, County Surveyor.

INDEX

	Page
An Historic Town	8
Albertson, I. D.	98
Albertson, John	98
Albertson, Early	98
Albertson, A. J.	98
Albertson, Ben	98
Albertson, John, Jr.	98
Allred, Theopholus	116
Anderson, Robert	126
Anderson, Tom	126
Anderson, Lewis	126
Allen, Fayette	28
Adkins, Dud	23
Burns, Mrs. Maggie	10
Bowden, E.	77
Bowden, John S.	108
Bowden, W. B.	77
Bowden, Joshua	78
Bowden, S. V.	78
Bowden, B. O.	79
Bowden, B. W.	80
Beaty, D. O.	81
Beaty, W. A.	91
Beaty, J. R.	91
Beaty, Andrew	91
Beaty, W. R.	94
Beaty, B. D.	109
Beaty, J. B.	115
Beaty, Tom	115
Beaty, Prime	115
Beaty, Lewis	115
Beaty, George W.	115
Beaty, C.	122
Beaty, James	115
Beaty, S. H.	152
Beaty, Jerry	152
Beaty, Putnam	152
Boles, G. H.	144
Boles, Gilbert	145
Bertram, Sam A.	127
Bertram, William	128
Big and Little Harp	133
Brier, A. L.	134

	Page
Brier, Albert	134
Brier, H. C.	135
Brier, Bertha	135
Blevins, Lake	150
Blevins, G. W.	150
Blevins, W. J.	158
Blevins, W. F.	146
Bledsoe, Scott	35
Bledsoe, Robert	35
Bledsoe, Bates	35
Bledsoe's Cavalry	22
Bledsoe's Company	21
Bentonville	32
Bradford, J. C.	152
Beaty's, Tinker, Company	37
Buck, J. T.	87
Buck, McPherson	103
Buttram, W. H.	154
Courthouse Plan by J. M. Clemons	12
Clemons, John M.	17
Chism, Dr. J. N.	80
Chism, L. B.	80
Cobb, Jesse	83
Cobb, Howell	83
Case, W. R.	90
Case, H. B.	90
Claiborne, M. D.	94
Claiborne, Stephen	94
Claiborne, Dr. R. T.	94
Claiborne, Leon	95
Conatser, G. W.	101
Conatser, John Palser	101
Conatser, Philip	101
Conatser, O. C.	156
Choate, Thomas	103
Clark, E. J.	146
Case, Hattie Love	117
Cravens, J. B.	118
Cravens, W. J.	118
Clay, Henry	118
Compton, J. H.	147
Choate, C. C.	118

INDEX

Name	Page	Name	Page
Crockett, W. M.	123	Fort Donelson	23
Crockett, Davy	63	Franklin, Battle of	23
Crockett, Jim	63	Following Sherman'to the Sea	32
Choate, Clark	127	Gaudin, John W.	84
Choate, Austin	127	Gaudin, W. J.	85
Cooper, G. W.	129	Greer, M. L.	88
Cooper, David	129	Greer, Sam	88
Cooper, Jacob	130	Greer, David	88
Cooper, Thomas	129	Greer, B. A.	120
Case, Prof. D. R.	135	Garrett, A. M.	89
Culver, L. D.	137	Garrett, J. L.	89
Culver, John	137	Garrett, Elijah	89
Culver, J. P.	137	Garrett, B. T.	122
Culver, Tom	137	Garrett, W. A.	157
Culver, M. M.	138	Garrett, Dr. I. L.	122
Colditz, Max	150	Gentry, John	110
Company "I" Officers	18	Gentry, W. M.	110
Company D, 8th Tenn. Cavalry	36	Gentry, David	110
Cruel Deeds	48	George, James	151
Davis, Dan	101	Gernt, Bruno	143
Delk, Sherwood	117	High School	11
Delk, David	117	Hood, J. A.	82
Delk, John	117	Hood, Sol	82
Delk, James	117	Hood, Elisha	82
Dowdy, Rufus	38	Hood, Andy	82
Ervin Hotel	9	Hood, Jerry	82
Erwin, Wade H.	114	Hood, Zeph	82
Evans, J. W.	83	Hood, John	82
Evans, Nathan	83	Hogue, Anderson	147
Edgefield, Battle of	23	Hogue, R. D.	158
East Tenn. Vol. Inf.	40	Hogue, J. A.	158
Fentress County	4	Hogue, Pleasant	143
Fentress County in War	18	Hogue, James R.	102
Fourth Tennessee Cavalry	18	Hogue, Sol	102
Bledsoe's Company	21	Hogue, D. E.	108
First Courthouse	12	Hogue, John R.	113
Frogge, C. C.	86	Hogue, A. R.	147
Frogge, O. O.	86	Hogue, Milburn	147
Frogge, J. W.	105	Hurst, M. F.	139
Frogge, John W.	86	Hickman, John P.	26
Frogge, S. E.	104	Hull, W. D.	141
Flecher, J. M.	96	Hull, Wm. D.	87
Flecher, Thomas D.	96	Hull, Cordell	119
Franklin, Jesse	154	Hull, Stanley	87
Franklin, G. W.	154	Hull, L. C.	110
Ferguson, Champ	30	Hall, C. M.	92

INDEX.

	Page		Page
Hall, Luke	92	Murfreesboro	22
Hall, David	92	McMinnville Recaptured	25
Hicks, John, Sr.	124	McCook Captured	27
Hicks, Joseph	125	Myers, Capt. C. E.	36
Harrison, G. E.	128	Morgan Captured	40
Home Guards	39	Muster Rolls, copies of	41-46
Hinds, Simeon	136	Obedstown	14
Hinds, George	136	Owen, Bailey	77
Hinds, Perry	136	Owen, Joshua	79
Hinds, John	136	Owen, Thomas	142
Indians	61	Owen, Elias	79
Indian Burial Grounds	132	Officers Union Army	41
Indian Wars	52	Pile, V. H.	97
Jamestown	8	Pile, S. H.	97
Johnson, P. E.	111	Pile, E.	97
Johnson, W. W.	111	Pile, R. C.	113
Johnson, John	111	Pile, W. M.	157
Johnson, Wayne	111	Pile, O. P.	155
Johnson, O. W.	111	Pile, J. L.	156
Johnson, J. N.	111	Pierce, S. B.	109
Jones, E. B.	152	Peavyhouse, A. A.	128
Kingston, Geo. S.	112	Peavyhouse, G. W.	128
Little, W. P.	96	Peavyhouse, Stanley H.	128
Loudon, Augustus	121	Price, Thurman	130
Loudon, Caroline	121	Price, Rev. Jasper	130
Lake, Stephens	149	Price, James	130
Masonic Hall	9	Price, Nathan	130
Mark Twain House	11	Price, Thos. D.	130
Mark Twain	14	Phillips, P. L.	151
Mullinix, Joe	103	Phillips, W. A.	151
Mullinix, Nathan	103	Phillips, Joe	151
Mullinix, W. D.	104	Phillips, W. R.	151
Mullinix, Isham	104	Potter, H.	157
Mullinix, Wm.	104	Potter, Thomas	157
Mullinix, W. E.	149	Potter, Cordell	157
Mullinix, Winton	149	Potter, Ibidell	157
Madewell, J. W.	88	Poor, John	28
Madewell, M. R.	88	Poor, Pleasant	28
McDonald, Martha Ellen (Smith)	99	Roysden, Miss Mary	94
Mexican War	56	Rankin, D. H.	99
Mitchell, Clyde C.	112	Rankin, Thomas	99
Millsaps, Marsha	65	Rankin, Robert	99
Millsaps, Capt. M. R.	37	Roysden, Jas. S.	103
Millsaps's Company	46	Rains, W. P.	116
Mace, A. J.	143	Rains, W. L.	116
McBroom, C. K.	153	Rains, Uriah	116

INDEX

Name	Page
Reagan, W. L.	118
Reagan, J. B.	125
Reagan, J. L.	125
Reagan, John	125
Reagan, Peter	125
Roberts, John A.	153
Roberts, A. H.	153
Roberts, Jesse	153
Richards, D. L.	143
Richards, John	143
Rodgers, R. H.	152
Reed, J. B.	156
Reed, Alonzo	157
Reagan, G. W.	157
Richardson, Steve, Killed	28
Roll Co. D, 1st Tenn.	42
Roll Other Companies	41-46
Revolutionary War	54
Stephens, R. J.	81
Stephens, David	81
Stephens, Isaiah	82
Stephens, Lottie	137
Stephens, Zorel	137
Sanders, F. O.	118
Storie, W. R.	90
Storie, A. J.	117
Storie, Wm. R.	90
Shearer, Daniel	99
Smith, Philip H.	139
Smith, George	123
Smith, Fred	110
Smith, A. S.	110
Smith, A. J.	118
Smith, Asa	120
Smith, David	120
Smith, Richard	120
Smith, James	120
Smith, D. D.	120
Smith, G. W.	123
Smith, Harve	124
Smith, Richard	124
Smith, G. T.	124
Smith, W. C.	141
Smith, W. J.	142
Stevens, John, Sr.	142
Smith, L. T.	146
Shelley, E. M.	108
Spanish-American War	56
Stewart, Rev. J. M.	100
Stockton, B. R.	131
Spurlin, M. H.	142
Simpson, J. N.	139
Story, J. W.	141
Sussner, Mrs. Ada	150
Snodgrass, C. E.	153
Sanders, F. O.	118
Taylor, Addie	93
Taylor, W. E.	102
Tinch, Frank	125
Todd, W. J.	150
Todd, Azariah	151
Turner, John	151
Tompkins, C. J.	158
Upchurch, Joe	157
Union Commanders	37
Voiles, Daniel	99
Voiles, William	99
Wright, Mathias	84
Wright, E. J.	105
Wright, J. F.	106
Wright, W. L.	106
Wright, Wm. L.	107
Wright, Boswell	106
Wright, Foster	107
Wright, Mack	107
Wright, J. C.	107
Wright, Ellen	107
Wright, Minnie	107
Wright, C. O.	108
Wright, Webster	108
Wright, Noble	108
Wright, Jacob	136
Wright, David	136
Wright, A. B.	154
Wright, W. D.	154
Wright, T. A.	155
Wright, Nelson	157
War of 1812	54
Williams, F. A.	93
Williams, Bertha	93
Williams, Sam	158
Williams, General	30

INDEX.

	Page		Page
Ward, J. D.	95	Wheeler, J. T.	121
Ward, James	95	Wheeler, Gen. Joe	18
Ward, George	95	Wheeler's Raid	25
Wilson, A. A.	112	Wheeler's Farewell Address	33
Wilson, Eli	112	Wood, D. V.	138
Wilson, George	112	Wood, W. W.	138
Winningham, S. W.	114	Wood, P. S.	156
Winningham, H. V.	120	Wood, Jerry	156
Winningham, R. A.	130	Young, Miss Ella A.	109
Winningham, W. S.	120	Young, W. D.	109
Winningham, Richard	130	York, Dr. P. C.	127
Winningham, Adam	131	York, Jeff	127
Welch, J. S.	116	York, James	127
Welch, Elijah	116		

www.ingramcontent.com/pod-product-compliance
Lightning Source LLC
Chambersburg PA
CBHW051100230426
43667CB00013B/2387